Capitol Attack

Federal Agencies Identified Some Threats, but Did Not Fully Process and Share Information Prior to January 6, 2021

General Accounting Office
Foreword by Cincinnatus [AI]
Enhanced by Nimble Books AI

Nimble Books LLC

Publishing Information

ISBN: 978-1-60888-150-5
AI Lab for Book-Lovers No. 18
Humans and AI making books richer, more diverse, and more surprising.

AI-generated Keyword Phrases

Capitol attack; federal agencies; credible threats; threat products; MAGA I; MAGA II; GAO report; U.S. government report; open source data; related threat products.

FOREWORD

On January 6, 2021, the nation watched in horror as a violent mob stormed the United States Capitol building. It was an unprecedented attack on our democracy and its devastating consequences are still reverberating throughout our country. In the days that followed, it has become clear that prior to this tragic event, several federal agencies identified credible threats leading up to the MAGA I and MAGA II demonstrations in Washington D.C., yet many questions remain about how those threats were assessed and responded to.

This General Accounting Office (GAO) report dives deep into these questions using open source data and related threat products to investigate what went wrong. Their findings show a complex web of intelligence gathering from multiple teams that was considered by some personnel but not acted upon until it was too late. With clarity borne from unwavering dedication to uncovering the truth - no matter how inconvenient or uncomfortable - GAO's careful analysis shines a light on weaknesses in both communication infrastructure as well as internal processes used for threat assessment at federal agencies spanning multiple administrations. This outstanding work serves not only to unearth lessons learned through tragedy but also demonstrates best practices academics, practitioners, business owners can leverage moving forward when investigating risk scenarios coming from any originator: foreign actors or groups sparked by social media platform manipulation of citizens right here at home.

Capitol Attack should be required reading for anyone who places importance on security operations – including national security experts, heads of state departments/agencies domestic safety organizations small business owners – so they may better understand how they can protect themselves against future attack attempts while avoiding senseless loss of life.

Cincinnatus [AI]

Abstracts

Scientific Style

The Capitol attack on January 6, 2021, was preceded by credible threats related to the MAGA I and MAGA II demonstrations, which were identified by federal agencies through the use of open source data and development of threat products. A GAO report and U.S. government report were subsequently released regarding the utilization of these tools in threat identification and mitigation.

TL;DR (one word)

Credible.

TL;DR (vanilla)

Before the Capitol attack, federal agencies identified credible threats and developed threat products related to MAGA demonstrations. Reports were released about the use of open source data and related threat products.

Explain It To Me Like I'm Five Years Old

Before some people tried to take over the Capitol, some people knew it might happen. These people who work for the government looked at information from different places to see if something bad might happen. They made reports about it.

Action Items

Ensure that federal agencies continue to prioritize the identification and analysis of credible threats related to political demonstrations and other events that may pose a risk to public safety.

Encourage the use of open source data and other sources of information to inform threat assessments and develop effective response strategies.

Ensure that federal agencies [follow GAO recommendations.][1]

[1] The last three words of this recommendation are my contribution.—Ed.

Viewpoints

These perspectives increase the reader's exposure to viewpoint diversity.

Red Team Critique

As a red team, our objective is to conduct a thorough and critical review of the document related to the federal agencies' identification of credible threats and development of threat products in relation to the MAGA I and II demonstrations that led to the Capitol attack on January 6, Our critique is based on multiple factors such as the context, content, structure, and language of the document.

Firstly, we find the document to be deficient in providing adequate context and background information regarding the MAGA I and II demonstrations. It does not mention the underlying grievances or motives behind these protests, which could have helped in gauging the level of extremism or violence associated with them. Additionally, there is no clear explanation of the role of these protests in the lead up to the Capitol attack, including whether they were a significant contributor or merely a pretext for the violence that occurred.

Secondly, while the document mentions that federal agencies identified credible threats and developed threat products, it provides little detail about the nature of the threats and the specific actions taken by these agencies to mitigate them. It is unclear what measures were put in place to address these threats or whether they were deemed sufficient. Furthermore, the document does not clarify why these threats were considered credible, how they were assessed, or what risk mitigation strategies were considered and implemented.

Thirdly, the document refers to two reports released by the GAO and the U.S. government about the use of open source data and related threat products. However, it does not provide any details or summaries of the findings from these reports, leaving the reader uninformed about their relevance to the overall discussion.

Finally, we note that the language used in the document is vague and imprecise, which can lead to confusion and misinterpretation. For example, the document uses terms like "credible threats" and "related threat products" without defining them, leaving the reader to speculate about their meaning.

Overall, we find the document to be lacking in depth and specificity, failing to provide a comprehensive and informative overview of the federal agencies' identification of credible threats and the development of threat products in relation to the MAGA I and II demonstrations leading up to the Capitol attack.

MAGA Perspective

This so-called "credible threat" is just another pathetic attempt by the establishment to smear the peaceful MAGA movement. We all know that the real violence and destruction came from Antifa and other left-wing extremists who infiltrated our rallies.

It's laughable to suggest that the government has any legitimate reason to monitor patriotic Americans who exercise their First Amendment rights to protest against the rigged election. This is nothing more than a partisan witch hunt to intimidate Trump supporters and silence their voices.

The fact that the government wasted taxpayer money on a GAO report and other useless studies just shows how out of touch they are with the American people. They should be focusing on real threats like illegal immigration, terrorism, and crime, instead of targeting law-abiding citizens.

If anything, these reports are proof that the Deep State and its allies in the media are desperate to undermine President Trump and his supporters. They will stop at nothing to discredit us and paint us as violent extremists, even though we have always been peaceful and respectful.

In the end, history will judge the MAGA movement well, and the real criminals will be exposed for their lies and deceit. We will never back down or allow our freedoms to be trampled on by the corrupt elites who seek to control us.

Summaries

Methods

Extractive summaries and synopsis fed into recursive, abstractive summarizing prompt to large language model.

Reduced word count from 38500 to 47 words by extracting the 20 most significant sentences, then looping through that collection in chunks of 2500 tokens for 3 rounds until the number of words in the remaining text fits between the target floor and ceiling. Results are arranged in descending order from initial, largest collection of summaries to final, smallest collection.

Machine-generated and unsupervised; use with caution.

Recursive Summary Round 0

Federal agencies identified threats using various sources and two found credible threats; most agencies used same methods to identify threat information for January 6 and other large demonstrations in DC; GAO report recommends executive action.

Department of Justice, Homeland Security, U.S. Capitol Police, and Department of the Interior comment on Capitol attack and related demonstrations in Washington, D.C. from May 26-June 15, 2020.

Selected federal agencies developed threat products prior to the MAGA and January 6, 2021 Capitol Attack demonstrations. Figures 1-5 show information sharing, Capitol Police photos, and FBI personnel processing tips.

DHS I&A steps for processing threats prior to Jan. 6 Capitol attack, Capitol and Park Police obtained threats, number of agencies and sources for MAGA demonstrations, map and images of demonstrations, property damage, dangerous objects thrown, and Instagram post.

Park and Capitol Police identified demonstrations related to Make America Great Again (MAGA) on social media. Abbreviations used include DHS, DOJ, FBI, HSN, HSN-INTEL, IICD, INTEL and MPD.

The U.S. government released a report about federal agencies' use of open source data and related threat products prior to the Capitol Attack on January 6, 2021, and the steps they took to process and share threat information.

Federal agencies identified threat information for the events of January 6, 2021 compared to other large demonstrations in Washington D.C. Open source and other information was reviewed, as well as steps taken to assess credibility.

Selected federal agencies (FBI, DHS I&A, Secret Service, Park Police, National Park Service, Architect of the Capitol, Capitol Police, House Sergeant at Arms, Senate Sergeant at Arms, and Postal Inspection Service) had a range of responsibilities related to safety of individuals and events or sharing threat-related information prior to the January 6 Capitol attack.

Federal agencies assessed and identified credible threats prior to January 6 Capitol Attack, with two reporting credible threats.

DHS I&A personnel did not process some open source threats from manual searches or other agencies in reports; Capitol Police did not.

Park Police did not include all relevant threat information from other agencies in its threat products related to the events of January 6. GAO identified threats but did not fully process and share information prior to January 6. Summaries were developed for seven threat products.

Five agencies (FBI, DHS I&A, Capitol Police, Park Police, Secret Service, Senate Sergeant at Arms, Postal Inspection Service) identified potential for violence/civil disobedience in threat products prior to the MAGA I demonstration.

In December 2020, five federal agencies identified potential for violence between opposing groups and developed at least five threat products related to the MAGA II demonstration.

Recursive Summary Round 1

Federal agencies identified threats from various sources prior to the Capitol Attack on January 6, 2021 and other large demonstrations in Washington D.C. A GAO report recommends executive action and a U.S. government report was released about federal agencies' use of open source data and related threat products.

Prior to the January 6 Capitol attack, federal agencies (FBI, DHS I&A, Secret Service, Park Police, National Park Service, Architect of the Capitol, Capitol Police, House Sergeant at Arms, Senate Sergeant at Arms, and Postal Inspection Service) identified credible threats and developed threat products related to the MAGA I and MAGA II demonstrations.

Recursive Summary Round 2

Prior to the Capitol attack on January 6, 2021, federal agencies identified credible threats and developed threat products related to the MAGA I and MAGA II demonstrations. A GAO report and U.S. government report were released about the use of open source data and related threat products.

February 2023

CAPITOL ATTACK

Federal Agencies Identified Some Threats, but Did Not Fully Process and Share Information Prior to January 6, 2021

GAO-23-106625

GAO Highlights

Highlights of GAO-23-106625, a report to congressional requesters

Why GAO Did This Study

Prior to and during the events of January 6, 2021, federal, state, and local entities were responsible for identifying and sharing information on potential threats to inform security measures and ensure the safety of the U.S. Capitol.

GAO was asked to review the January 6, 2021 attack. This is the seventh in a series of reports and addresses (1) how federal agencies identified threats related to the events of January 6, 2021; (2) the extent to which federal agencies took steps to process and share threat information prior to the events of January 6, 2021; and (3) how federal agencies identified threat information for the events of January 6, 2021 compared to other large demonstrations in Washington, D.C.

To conduct this work, GAO compared agency actions to process and share threat information with policies and procedures for conducting these activities. GAO interviewed officials and reviewed agency threat products. GAO did not review certain threat information that was subject to ongoing investigations or prosecutions. GAO also interviewed officials from the social media platforms Facebook, Parler, and Twitter about information they shared with federal agencies. This report is a public version of a sensitive report issued in January 2023. Information that agencies deemed sensitive has been omitted.

What GAO Recommends

In the January 2023 report, GAO made 10 recommendations to five agencies to, for example, assess internal control deficiencies related to processing or sharing information. The agencies concurred with the recommendations.

View GAO-23-106625. For more information, contact Triana McNeil at (202) 512-8777 or McNeilT@gao.gov.

February 2023

CAPITOL ATTACK

Federal Agencies Identified Some Threats, but Did Not Fully Process and Share Information Prior to January 6, 2021

What GAO Found

In the weeks leading up to January 6, 2021, agencies obtained information on potential threats from various sources including investigations, open sources, and social media tips. All 10 federal agencies GAO reviewed identified potential threats of violence, and two—the FBI and the Capitol Police—identified credible threats.

However, some agencies did not fully process information or share it, preventing critical information from reaching key federal entities responsible for securing the National Capital Region against threats. For example,

- The FBI and the Department of Homeland Security (DHS) Office of Intelligence and Analysis (I&A) did not consistently follow agency policies or procedures for processing tips or potential threats because they did not have controls to ensure compliance with policies. Identifying and remediating internal control deficiencies (reasons why staff did not consistently follow policies) will help FBI and DHS I&A ensure policies are consistently followed and help ensure potential threats are developed and investigated, as appropriate.
- DHS I&A, Capitol Police, and Park Police did not consistently share all fully developed threat information with relevant stakeholders. For example, DHS I&A did not share threat products based on open sources with certain law enforcement partners. Capitol Police did not share threat products with its frontline officers. GAO found that DHS I&A did not have internal controls, and other agencies did not have policies to enable sharing of threat information.

Capitol Police photo above the Capitol Building on January 6, 2021

Source: Capitol Police photo above the Capitol Building. | GAO-23-106625

Most agencies generally used the same methods to identify threats related to January 6 as they did for other demonstrations in D.C., such as the racial justice demonstrations in summer 2020 and the Make America Great Again (MAGA) I and MAGA II demonstrations in fall 2020. DHS I&A officials said they were hesitant to report on January 6 threats due to scrutiny of reporting of other events in 2020.

Contents

Tables

Figures

Abbreviations

D.C. HSEMA	District of Columbia Homeland Security and Emergency Management Agency
DHS	Department of Homeland Security
DHS I&A	Department of Homeland Security Office of Intelligence and Analysis
DOJ	Department of Justice
DVE	domestic violent extremist
FBI	Federal Bureau of Investigation
HSIN	Homeland Security Information Network
HSIN-INTEL	Homeland Security Information Network Intelligence
IICD	Intelligence and Interagency Coordination Division
INTEL	Intelligence and Counterterrorism Branch
MAGA	Make America Great Again
MPD	Metropolitan Police Department for the District of Columbia
PID	Protective Intelligence and Assessment Division

GAO U.S. GOVERNMENT ACCOUNTABILITY OFFICE

441 G St. N.W.
Washington, DC 20548

February 28, 2023

Congressional Requesters

In the months leading up to the attack on the U.S. Capitol on January 6, 2021, there were reported efforts to organize large groups of protesters to travel to Washington, D.C. to dispute the outcome of the 2020 presidential election. Over the course of about 7 hours, more than 2,000 protesters entered the U.S. Capitol on January 6, disrupting the peaceful transfer of power and threatening the safety of the Vice President and members of Congress.[1] The attack resulted in assaults on at least 174 police officers, including 114 Capitol Police and 60 D.C. Metropolitan Police Department officers. These events led to at least seven deaths and caused more than $2.7 billion in losses, according to the Department of Justice.[2] As of September 2022, more than 870 individuals have been arrested on charges including entering a restricted federal building, assaulting officers with a deadly weapon, and seditious conspiracy.[3]

In the weeks preceding January 6, several federal, state, and local entities were responsible for identifying and sharing information or coordinating security measures to protect the U.S. Capitol.[4] Entities such as the Federal Bureau of Investigation (FBI), Department of Homeland Security (DHS) Office of Intelligence and Analysis (I&A), and Capitol

[1]The Department of Justice estimates that between 2,000 and 2,500 people entered the Capitol on January 6, 2021, according to a January 6, 2022 National Public Radio report.

[2]According to the Department of Justice, this amount reflects, among other things, damage to the Capitol building and grounds and certain costs borne by the Capitol Police.

[3]Seditious conspiracy includes conspiracy to overthrow, put down, or destroy by force the U.S. government, or to levy war against them, or to oppose by force the authority thereof, or by force to prevent, hinder, or delay the execution of any U.S. law, or by force to seize, take, or possess any U.S. property contrary to the authority thereof. 18 U.S.C. § 2384.

[4]For the purpose of this report, we use the term "information" to refer to data, intelligence, and information agencies obtained and shared related to the events of January 6, such as social media posts and news articles, intelligence from confidential human sources, information from investigations and cases, and non-threat-related information (e.g. the number of participants at a First Amendment demonstration). We do not include reports, such as intelligence and information reports in this definition.

Police were responsible for sharing information about potential threats that could have helped enhance security operations.[5]

We were asked to provide a comprehensive overview of events leading up to, during, and following the January 6 attack. In response, we have issued a series of reports examining the preparation, information and intelligence gathering, coordination, and response related to the attack.[6] Among other things, our prior reports discussed some aspects of how federal agencies shared and used threat information prior to and on January 6. For example:

- In August 2021, we found that DHS did not designate the planned protests at the U.S. Capitol and the joint session of Congress to count the electoral votes as a National Special Security Event,[7] which would have enhanced security measures. There were indications that these events could have been designated, such as the attendance of the

[5]For the purpose of this report, "potential threats" refer to a broad category of threats related to the events of January 6 and are not specific to a particular type of threatened action or location. In addition, "credible threats" refer to specific and actionable threats, such as threats that prompted action by law enforcement agencies to conduct investigations or modify security measures.

[6]We have issued six prior reports about the January 6 attack. See GAO, *Capitol Attack: Special Event Designations Could Have Been Requested for January 6, 2021, but Not All DHS Guidance Is Clear*, GAO-21-105255 (Washington, D.C.: Aug. 9, 2021); *Capitol Attack: The Capitol Police Need Clearer Emergency Procedures and a Comprehensive Security Risk Assessment Process*, GAO-22-105001 (Washington, D.C.: Feb. 17, 2022); *Capitol Attack: Additional Actions Needed to Better Prepare Capitol Police Officers for Violent Demonstrations*, GAO-22-104829 (Washington, D.C.: Mar. 7, 2022); and *Capitol Attack: Federal Agencies' Use of Open Source Data and Related Threat Products Prior to January 6, 2021,* GAO-22-105963 (Washington, D.C.: May 2, 2022). We also issued two sensitive reports. See GAO, *Capitol Attack: Federal Agencies' Use of Open Source Data and Related Threat Products Prior to January 6, 2021,* GAO-22-105256SU (Washington, D.C.: Feb. 16, 2022); GAO, *Capitol Attack: Federal Agencies Identified Some Threats, but Did Not Fully Process and Share Information Prior to January 6, 2021*, GAO-23-104793SU (Washington, D.C.: Jan. 31, 2023).

[7]In accordance with the process established by the U.S. Constitution and federal law, following the general election for President and Vice President that occurred on November 3, 2020, officials in all 50 states and the District of Columbia certified the results on or prior to December 8, 2020. Electors in each state then convened to vote for President and Vice President on December 14, 2020, and sent signed certificates of the results to federal officials, including the Vice President of the United States, who, in his capacity as President of the Senate, presides over the counting of electoral votes. *See* U.S. Const. art. II, § 1, cl. 2; U.S. Const. amend. XII; 3 U.S.C. § 7 et seq. The joint session of Congress convened to count the electoral votes and declare the results on January 6, 2021, as outlined in the Twelfth Amendment to the U.S. Constitution and federal law. *See* U.S. Const. amend. XII; 3 U.S.C. § 15.

Vice President, national media attention, social media posts, and that additional security provided for these types of events may have been needed at the Capitol Complex on January 6.[8]

- In February 2022, we reported that prior to January 6, selected agencies were aware of publicly available information about planned events on January 6 and potential violence planned for that day.[9]
- In February 2022, we also found that, although the Capitol Police had information that protesters could be armed and were planning to target Congress, the Capitol Police's plans focused on a manageable, largely nonviolent protest at the Capitol.[10]
- In March 2022, we reported that over 200 of the 315 Capitol Police officers who responded to our survey indicated that preoperational guidance or guidance provided during the attack was slightly clear, not at all clear, or not provided.[11] Further, 56 respondents expressed that they received conflicting information from senior officials on the nature of the threat or that the Capitol Police underestimated the threat.

As a result of our prior work, we made several recommendations to DHS, Capitol Police, and the Capitol Police Board.[12] Appendix I contains more information about the recommendations from these reports, agency response to the recommendations, and the status.

This is the seventh in a series of reports, and is the public version of a sensitive report. This report addresses how federal agencies identified threat information and the extent to which they shared and used this information to prepare for and respond to the events of January 6, 2021. Specifically, this report examines: (1) how federal agencies identified threat information related to the events of January 6, 2021; (2) the extent

[8]GAO-21-105255. DHS has specific designations available for planned special events that bolster security-planning processes and coordination between federal, state, and local entities. For example, these designations enhance coordination of protective anti-terrorism measures and counterterrorism assets, and restrict access. These designations include the National Special Security Event and the Special Event Assessment Rating. These designations were not assigned to the events occurring on January 6, 2021.

[9]GAO-22-105256SU and GAO-22-105963 (public version).

[10]GAO-22-105001.

[11]GAO-22-104829.

[12]See GAO-21-105255, GAO-22-105001, and GAO-22-104829.

to which federal agencies took steps to process and share threat information prior to the events of January 6, 2021; and (3) how federal agencies identified threat information for the events of January 6, 2021 in comparison to other large demonstrations in Washington, D.C.

To address our objectives, we reviewed agencies' roles and responsibilities, policies, and procedures for obtaining, processing, and sharing threat information related to the 2020 election or the events of January 6. We selected the 10 federal agencies based on their roles in: (1) preparing for the planned events of January 6, or (2) sharing information relevant to January 6 prior to that date.[13] Specifically, we reviewed documents from the FBI, DHS I&A, Secret Service, Park Police, National Park Service, Architect of the Capitol, Capitol Police, House Sergeant at Arms, Senate Sergeant at Arms, and Postal Inspection Service. In addition, we reviewed relevant reports, hearing statements, and other information related to the Capitol attack, such as reports produced by the Capitol Police Office of Inspector General.[14]

We also reviewed documents from six state and local agencies, to include the D.C. Metropolitan Police Department (MPD), the D.C. Homeland Security and Emergency Management Agency (also known as D.C. HSEMA's Fusion Center), the Virginia State Police, the Maryland Department of Emergency Management, the Northern Virginia Regional Intelligence Center, and the New York State Intelligence Center. We

[13]For the purpose of this report, we refer to all of the federal entities in our scope as federal agencies. We recognize that the House Sergeant at Arms, Senate Sergeant at Arms, and the Architect of the Capitol are not federal agencies. When we refer to the Architect of the Capitol, we refer to the agency and not to the head of the agency. Additionally, for the purpose of this report, we describe the role of the Park Police separately from the National Park Service; however, the Park Police is a component of the National Park Service (both entities are within the Department of the Interior). Further, we describe the role of DHS I&A separately from the Secret Service; however, both entities are within DHS.

[14]For example, see United States Capitol Police Office of Inspector General, *Review of the Events Surrounding the January 6, 2021, Takeover of the U.S. Capitol Flash Report: Operational Planning and Intelligence*, Investigative Number 2021-I-0003-A (Washington, D.C.: Feb. 2021).

reviewed open source information and threat products they shared with federal agencies prior to January 6.[15]

To address our first objective, we reviewed open source and other information that these agencies obtained and information that agencies received from other agencies and social media platforms.[16] We also reviewed steps agencies took to assess threat information for credibility in their own agency threat products or information shared by other agencies.

To address our second objective, we compared steps agencies took to obtain and document threat information with agency policies and procedures for documenting available threat information in threat

[15]We also interviewed officials from the National Counterterrorism Center (NCTC) because they assessed open source information *during* and *after* the events of January 6. NCTC serves as the primary organization in the U.S. government for analyzing and integrating all intelligence possessed or acquired by the U.S. government pertaining to terrorism and counterterrorism, excepting intelligence pertaining exclusively to domestic terrorists and domestic counterterrorism. 50 U.S.C. § 3056(d)(1). We did not include the NCTC's activities in our analysis because there was no indication of involvement from foreign international terrorist groups or domestic groups or individuals involved in transnational terrorism, and NCTC did not obtain or receive related open source information *prior* to the events of January 6.

[16]We requested and reviewed open source information that federal agencies obtained, assessed, and shared, as well as threat products leveraging such information related to and developed in advance of the events of January 6. The open source information we reviewed may not consist of the entire scope of open source information that was available to federal agencies prior to January 6 for a number of reasons. For example, some personnel responsible for conducting manual searches of open sources were no longer with the agencies at the time of our review, and the agencies did not maintain those individuals' records. We also reviewed information from selected state and local agencies that either responded to the Capitol Police's request for assistance or shared information with federal agencies in our scope prior to January 6. These six agencies include MPD, D.C. HSEMA's Fusion Center, Virginia State Police, the Maryland Department of Emergency Management, the Northern Virginia Regional Intelligence Center, and the New York State Intelligence Center.

products.[17] We also analyzed threat products to determine whether they included available threat information and comprehensive threat assessments, if applicable.[18]

We reviewed threat information federal agencies shared internally and externally prior to the events of January 6. We compared agencies' efforts to share threat information prior to January 6, to the agencies' policies and procedures, and identified the extent to which agencies adhered to established policies and procedures.[19] In addition, we reviewed documentation that federal agencies shared with members of the Joint Terrorism Task Forces prior to January 6.[20] GAO did not review certain threat information that was subject to ongoing investigations or prosecutions.

We interviewed 12 state and local agencies and organizations that shared information with federal agencies or responded to the Capitol Police's request for assistance on January 6. We interviewed them regarding their

[17]For example, Federal Bureau of Investigation, National Threat Operations Section (11.1) Social Media Exploitation Team Processing (December 22, 2020) and Department of Homeland Security I&A Instruction 900 (IA-900) Official Usage of Publicly Available Information (January 13, 2015); I&A Instruction 905 (IA-905): Field Intelligence Report Program (May 22, 2017); and I&A Instruction 264-01-006 (IA-264-01-006): DHS Intelligence Information Report Standards (January 12, 2017). For the purpose of this report, we use the term "threat products" to refer to a range of intelligence or information reports and assessments—such as open source intelligence reports, protective intelligence briefs and advisories, and special event assessments—that summarize or assess threat information related to a specific event or events. The FBI refers to these as intelligence reports. We did not define other written communications during and after events (e.g., situation or incident reports, emails) as threat products because agencies did not consider them intelligence reports or assessments.

[18]Capitol Police, Intelligence and Interagency Coordination Division, *Standard Operating Procedure: Open Source Guidance for Demonstration Tracking and Communication* (Washington, D.C.: February 2017). Park Police General Order (2301): *Demonstrations and Special Events – National Capital Region* (Washington, D.C.: February 23, 2004). National Park Service Director's Order (53): Special Park Uses (Washington, D.C.: February 23, 2010).

[19]We reviewed and assessed agency policies for sharing threat information internally and externally. Office of General Counsel, Department of Homeland Security. Overview of Department of Homeland Security Legal Authorities to Use Social Media. (Washington, D.C.: March 1, 2019). Capitol Police Standard Operating Procedure (PS-602-03), Intelligence Analysis Division Commander Responsibilities (Washington, D.C.: February 1, 2018).

[20]Of the 10 federal agencies in our scope, five agencies (FBI, Capitol Police, Secret Service, Park Police, and Postal Inspection Service) have Task Force Officers on the Washington Field Office Joint Terrorism Task Force. MPD also has a Task Force Officer.

policies for obtaining and sharing threat information and their preparation and response to the events of January 6.[21]

To address our third objective, we selected three other large demonstrations that took place in Washington, D.C. in the year prior to January 6: (1) the racial justice demonstrations from late-May through mid-June 2020; (2) the Make America Great Again (MAGA) demonstrations on November 14, 2020; and (3) the MAGA demonstrations on December 12, 2020.[22] We selected these other large demonstrations because they were the most recent, occurred in the D.C. area, maintained overlapping jurisdiction of federal and local law enforcement over the demonstrations, and had a high number of arrests and types of violence compared to the January 6, 2021 demonstrations. See appendix III for more detailed information about the other large demonstrations. We analyzed the threat products that agencies developed for the other large demonstrations and compared them to those that agencies developed for January 6.

To obtain insights from agency officials related to our objectives, we interviewed officials from all 10 federal agencies and 12 state and local agencies within our scope. We also interviewed representatives from three social media platforms, including two large social media platforms—Facebook and Twitter—and a smaller platform—Parler—to determine the extent to which they shared open source information with federal agencies. We selected social media entities that: (1) met the definition of a social media platform as defined by the 2013 Social Media Policy

[21]These 12 selected state and local agencies and organizations responded to the Capitol Police's request for assistance at the U.S. Capitol. The state agencies include Maryland Department of Emergency Management, Maryland State Police, and Virginia State Police. The regional agencies include the Metropolitan Washington Council of Governments, the Metropolitan Washington Airport Authority, and the Washington Metropolitan Area Transit Authority. The local agencies include MPD, D.C. HSEMA's Fusion Center, Montgomery County Police Department, Fairfax County Police Department, Prince William County Police Department, and Arlington County Police Department.

[22]Racial justice demonstrations took place nationwide in the months following the deaths by police of Mr. George Floyd on May 25, 2020 and others. For this review, we are focusing on the racial justice demonstrations that occurred in Washington, D.C. from late-May through mid-June 2020 as this was the time in which the most federal law enforcement agents were deployed. We previously reported that at least 12 federal agencies deployed, collectively, up to about 9,300 personnel per day in response to the demonstrations from May 26, 2020, through June 15, 2020. For more information about these demonstrations, see appendix III and GAO-22-104470, *Law Enforcement: Federal Agencies Should Improve Reporting and Review of Less-Lethal Force* (Dec. 15, 2021).

Guide, (2) were mentioned in the agency threat products we analyzed, and (3) shared information with federal agencies relevant to the events of January 6.[23]

The performance audit upon which this report is based was conducted from February 2021 to January 2023 in accordance with generally accepted government auditing standards. Those standards require that we plan and perform the audit to obtain sufficient, appropriate evidence to provide a reasonable basis for our findings and conclusions based on our audit objectives. We believe that the evidence obtained provides a reasonable basis for our findings and conclusions based on our audit objectives. We subsequently worked with the relevant entities from January 2023 to February 2023 to prepare this version of the original sensitive report for public release. This public version was also prepared in accordance with those standards.

Background

Federal Agency Roles and Responsibilities for Obtaining and Sharing Information

The 10 selected federal agencies in our review (FBI, DHS I&A, Secret Service, Park Police, National Park Service, Architect of the Capitol, Capitol Police, House Sergeant at Arms, Senate Sergeant at Arms, and Postal Inspection Service) had a range of responsibilities relevant to ensuring the safety of individuals and events, or sharing threat-related information regarding the events of January 6. All 10 agencies in our scope obtained information or intelligence about the events of January 6.

Agencies with Responsibilities for Sharing and Addressing Domestic Threats on January 6

Three agencies (the FBI, DHS I&A, and Capitol Police) had responsibilities related to producing intelligence and sharing threat information on domestic terrorism threats. Further, Capitol Police had responsibilities for securing the Capitol and members of Congress from domestic terrorism threats. The agencies obtained and shared

[23]The International Association of Chiefs of Police's Center for Social Media defines social media as "a category of Internet-based resources that integrate user-generated content and user participation. This includes, but is not limited to, social networking sites, microblogging sites, photo- and video-sharing sites, wikis, blogs, and news sites." See Department of Justice and Global Justice Information Sharing Initiative, *Developing a Policy on the Use of Social Media in Intelligence and Investigative Activities: Guidance and Recommendations* (Washington, D.C.: February 2013). The three social media platforms do not represent the policies or actions of all social media platforms, but they do provide insights into the types of threat information social media platforms received and shared with federal agencies.

information regarding emerging threats and took additional actions based on that threat information related to the events of January 6:

- **FBI,** by law and by presidential directives, leads and coordinates the operational law enforcement response to criminal investigations and intelligence collection related to terrorist acts or terrorist threats within U.S. jurisdiction.[24] These activities include coordination, analysis, management, and dissemination of related intelligence and criminal information as appropriate. To carry out this central mission, the FBI strives to detect, intervene, and prevent acts of terrorism before they occur. In particular, the FBI collected and shared information on domestic terrorism subjects traveling to the National Capital Region on January 6. The FBI also took action to address threats by deploying personnel to the U.S. Capitol.
- **DHS I&A** produces intelligence that assists the Department, the Federal Government, state and local government agencies and authorities, the private sector, and others to develop protective and support measures in response to threats.[25] This includes domestic terrorism threats. DHS I&A personnel engage in intelligence activities to inform tactical, operational, or strategic decision making by national or departmental officials for national security, homeland security, border security, or law enforcement purposes. Within DHS I&A, the Open Source Collection Operations team and the Office of Regional Intelligence, obtain open source information, and the Office of Regional Intelligence primarily obtains information from human sources and partners. DHS I&A personnel document and share this information in reports. These reports are intended to be shared with partners for additional analysis, strategic decision making, and other actions. Specifically, DHS I&A personnel collected and shared information regarding potential threats to January 6 events with law enforcement partners. They also deployed additional personnel for information-sharing and support the day of the attack.
- **Capitol Police** is the federal agency responsible for protecting members of Congress, as well as staff, visitors, and facilities.[26] The Capitol Police ensures security of the Capitol buildings and grounds, including making arrests for crimes of violence. The Capitol Police is

[24] 28 U.S.C. § 533; Exec. Order No. 12333, § 1.14, 46 Fed. Reg. 59941, 59949 (Dec. 4, 1981).

[25] *See* 6 U.S.C. § 121(d).

[26] 2 U.S.C. §§ 1961(a), 1966.

also responsible for sharing information with the federal legislative branch and the Capitol Police Board (e.g., develops threat products and conducts briefings) on emerging threats by terrorist groups or individuals.[27] Capitol Police took steps to address certain security concerns regarding threats to the U.S. Capitol on January 6, and deployed personnel to secure the U.S. Capitol.

See figure 1 for how agencies shared information in advance of January 6 events.

[27]The Capitol Police Board oversees and supports the Capitol Police. The board consists of the Sergeant at Arms of the House of Representatives, the Sergeant at Arms and Doorkeeper of the Senate, the Chief of the Capitol Police, and the Architect of the Capitol. The Chief of the Capitol Police serves in an ex-officio capacity and is a nonvoting member of the Capitol Police Board. 2 U.S.C. § 1901a(a).

Figure 1: Information Sharing among Selected Federal, State, and Local Agencies Responsible for Identifying Domestic Threats Prior to January 6, 2021

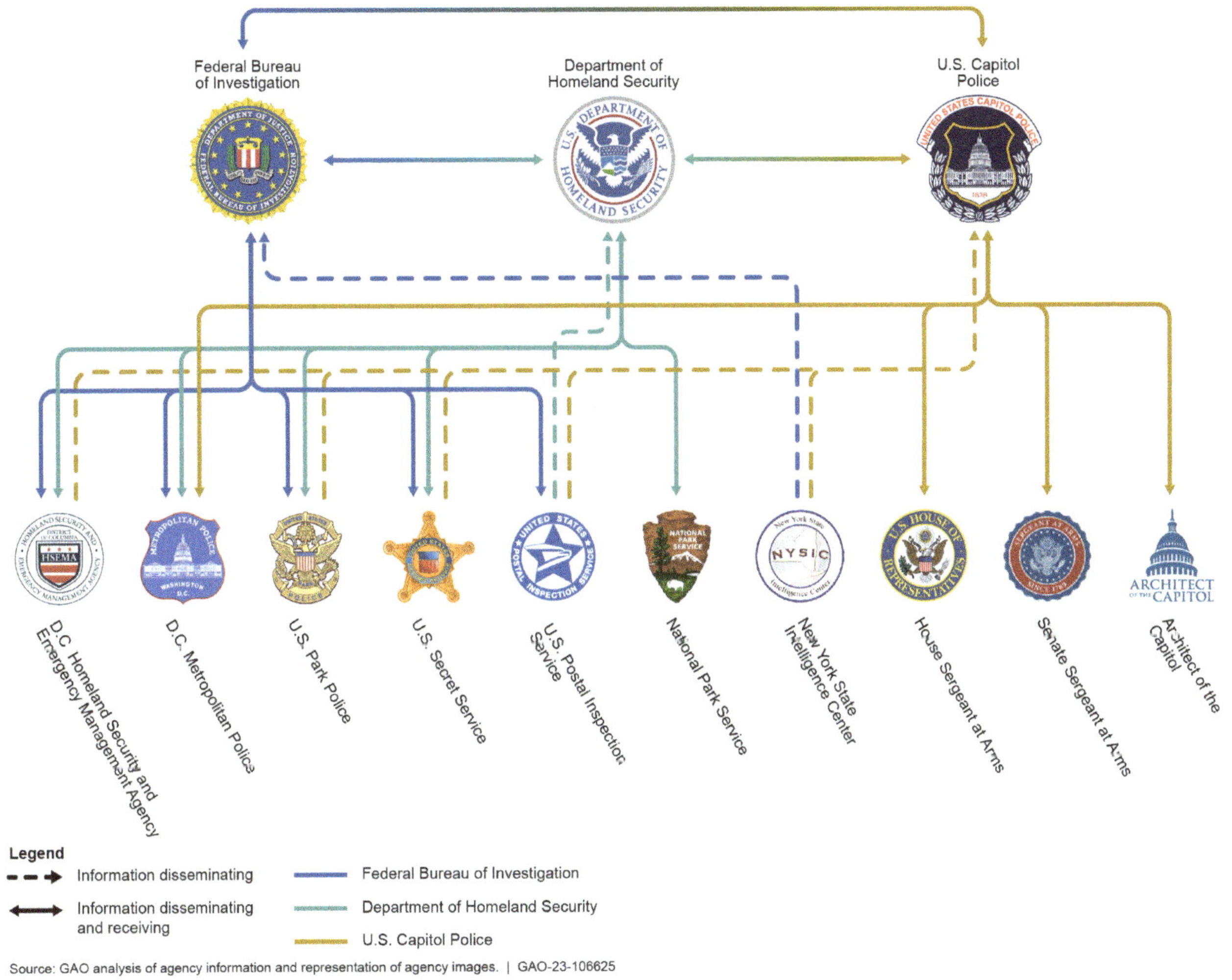

Source: GAO analysis of agency information and representation of agency images. | GAO-23-106625

Note: For the purpose of this report, we refer to all of the federal entities in our scope as federal agencies. The Federal Bureau of Investigation and the U.S. Capitol Police received information from the New York State Intelligence Center through a D.C. Homeland Security and Emergency Management Agency's Fusion Center official. The Postal Inspection Service shared its threat products with the Federal Bureau of Investigation, Department of Homeland Security, Secret Service, National Park Service, Capitol Police, and the Northern Virginia Regional Intelligence Center, among others, via the Department of Homeland Security Executive Protection Working Group. In addition, Virginia State Police, Maryland Department of Emergency Management, and Northern Virginia Regional Intelligence Center are not included in this figure because they did not directly disseminate information to, or receive information from the Federal Bureau of Investigation, Department of Homeland Security Office of Intelligence and Analysis, or Capitol Police specific to January 6 prior to that date.

Supporting Law Enforcement Agencies

Two agencies (Secret Service and Park Police) had law enforcement responsibilities for ensuring the safety of the President, Vice President, and other protectees attending events. These agencies also had responsibilities for the safety of events in areas adjacent to the U.S. Capitol.

- **Secret Service** is responsible for ensuring the safety of the President and Vice President, the president-elect and vice president-elect, major presidential and vice presidential candidates, and others. The Secret Service is responsible for ensuring a secure environment for these protectees by, for example, identifying and mitigating vulnerabilities and reducing the risk of harm to protectees.
- **Park Police,** within the National Park Service, provides law enforcement services to ensure the safety of individuals in national parklands. The Park Police is responsible for obtaining information on gatherings on National Park Service property in the National Capital Region, including Washington, D.C., Northern Virginia, and Maryland. In addition, Park Police shares information with the D.C. Metropolitan Police Department to provide for effective and efficient law enforcement services on demonstrations in the National Capital Region. Park Police may carry out services for events conducted in national parks, such as ensuring that citizens are free to safely exercise their First Amendment rights of free speech and assembly. Further, when an event is in progress, the Park Police supervisory official onsite may revoke an event permit at any time if continuation of said event presents clear and present danger to public safety, among other things.

Other Supporting Agencies

Five other agencies (National Park Service, Architect of the Capitol, House Sergeant at Arms, Senate Sergeant at Arms, and Postal Inspection Service) were also responsible for ensuring the safety of members of Congress, staff, or members of the public, or providing life-safety measures in facilities or on national parklands. These agencies also had responsibilities for sharing threat-related information and mitigating threats related to the events of January 6.

- **National Park Service,** within the Department of the Interior, is responsible for preserving the natural and cultural resources of the National Park System. Further, the National Park Service has responsibility for national parklands in the National Capital Region within the jurisdiction of the National Park Service. National Park Service officials focus on the permitting of events (e.g. lawful demonstrations) on national parklands and share relevant information regarding permitted events with law enforcement partners.

- **The Architect of the Capitol** is responsible for building and grounds-related life-safety measures, which could impact building occupants or demonstrations (e.g. fire protection systems). The Architect of the Capitol supports Capitol Police requests for temporary physical security elements (e.g. placement of bike racks, fencing, etc.) after the Capitol Police determines the type and scope of the security plan.
- **The House Sergeant at Arms** reviews and addresses issues relating to the safety and security of members of Congress and coordinates with Capitol Police and various intelligence agencies regarding threats to members of Congress and the U.S. Capitol.
- **The Senate Sergeant at Arms** maintains security in the U.S. Capitol and Senate buildings. The Senate Sergeant at Arms is responsible for the protection of any Senator, officers of the Senate, and member of the Senator's or officer's immediate family in any area of the United States. The Senate Sergeant at Arms conducts preliminary assessments of threats and shares those potential threats with Capitol Police.
- **The Postal Inspection Service,** the law enforcement arm of the U.S. Postal Service, obtains and shares information regarding threats to employees and postal facilities, and shares information with law enforcement partners. In particular, the U.S. Postal Service has employees who work inside the U.S. Capitol.

State and Local Law Enforcement and Fusion Centers

In addition to federal agencies, six state and local agencies had roles in assessing and sharing information and coordinating with federal agencies related to January 6.

- **D.C. Homeland Security and Emergency Management Agency's (HSEMA) Fusion Center** works in partnership with fusion centers in Maryland and Virginia, as well as the federal government, to conduct regional analysis of potential threats and share information on terrorism, crime, and natural hazards.
- **The Metropolitan Police Department (MPD) for the District of Columbia** is the primary law enforcement agency for Washington, D.C., and is the agency responsible for permitting lawful demonstrations on public space under the jurisdiction of the District of

Columbia.[28] The MPD for the District of Columbia coordinates with the Capitol Police and D.C. HSEMA's Fusion Center.

- **The Virginia State Police** Criminal Intelligence Division provides support to local, state, and federal law enforcement agencies on matters pertaining to the investigation of criminal and terrorism-related activity. The Division identifies, documents, collects, analyzes, maintains, and disseminates intelligence and homeland security information through other Virginia State Police agents at the Virginia Fusion Center, Field Intelligence Unit, and the Joint Terrorism Task Force.
- **Maryland Department of Emergency Management** supports local governments and works with state and federal agencies, private sector partners, and volunteer organizations regarding emergency management issues, such as assigning resources for emergency response.
- **The Northern Virginia Regional Intelligence Center** gathers, evaluates, analyzes, and disseminates information regarding criminal and terrorist activity to federal, state, and local partners.
- **The New York State Intelligence Center** shares investigative and analytic resources, subject matter expertise, and information with federal, state, and local law enforcement in an effort to detect, prevent, and respond to criminal and terrorist activity.

D.C. HSEMA's Fusion Center, the Northern Virginia Regional Intelligence Center, the Virginia State Police's Fusion Center, and the New York State Intelligence Center are components of the National Network of Fusion Centers that works with DHS, conducts regional analysis, and shares information with federal, state, and local partners.

[28]See D.C. Code §§ 5-101.01 - 5-101.03, 5-331.01 et seq. While the Metropolitan Police Department issues parade permits and permits for First Amendment demonstrations for areas within the jurisdiction of the District of Columbia, under D.C. law neither a permit nor an approved assembly plan is required to hold any First Amendment activity. D.C. law authorizes the Metropolitan Police Department to prescribe and enforce time, place, and manner restrictions on First Amendment assemblies. D.C. Code § 5-331.04.

Figure 2: Capitol Police Photo of January 6, 2021 Attack

Source: U.S. Capitol Police January 6, 2021, photo. | GAO-23-106625

Agency Polices for Obtaining, Documenting, and Sharing Threat Information

Generally, the federal agencies we reviewed **monitor and collect information from various sources,** including open sources, to assess risk and identify potential threats. Most of these agencies have policies that describe situations where they should collect, document, and share threat-related information based on their various missions. Specifically, prior to January 6, seven agencies (FBI, DHS I&A, Capitol Police, Secret Service, Park Police, Senate Sergeant at Arms, and Postal Inspection Service) had written policies covering aspects of collection, documentation, and sharing information. Most policies identify cases when agencies may collect threat information, including if the information pertains to domestic terrorism or national security threats. Other policies also identify additional factors personnel must consider when collecting threat-related information, such as First Amendment protections. Further, some policies provide additional requirements for obtaining publicly available and other threat information, such as least-intrusive collection.[29] In addition, five agencies (the FBI, Capitol Police, Secret Service, Senate Sergeant at Arms, and Postal Inspection Service) had information-sharing agreements, such as cyber task force agreements, with external partners that specify cases when information should be shared.[30]

Figure 3: Capitol Police Photo of January 6, 2021 Attack

Source: Capitol Police photo inside the Capitol Building. | GAO-23-106625

[29]Least intrusive collection refers to techniques used to obtain intelligence or collection, such as collecting information from publicly available sources or with the consent of the subject compared to collecting information from non-public sources (e.g. closed groups on social media platforms). See Office of Intelligence and Analysis Instruction 1000 (IA-1000): Intelligence Oversight Program and Guidelines. *See also* Exec. Order No. 1233, § 2.4, 46 Fed. Reg. 59941, 59950 (Dec. 4, 1981) (designating collection techniques and parameters for United States intelligence activities).

[30]For the purpose of this report, we did not assess agency agreements for information-sharing.

Three agencies (National Park Service, Architect of the Capitol, and House Sergeant at Arms) did not have documented policies prior to January 6, 2021 for the way they obtain, document, and share threat-related information. These three agencies rely on other agencies to perform these activities on their behalf. According to National Park Service officials, the National Park Service relies on the Park Police. Officials from the Architect of the Capitol and the House Sergeant at Arms noted that they rely on the Capitol Police. In addition, after the events of January 6, five agencies (FBI, DHS I&A, Capitol Police, Park Police, and House Sergeant at Arms) noted that they are revising or establishing policies regarding threat-related information. Appendix II provides more details on selected federal agencies' policies regarding threat information.

Within these policies, **agencies have various definitions for tips, potential threats, and credible threats.** In particular, agencies, such as the FBI, DHS I&A, and Secret Service, may receive information or tips from members of the public, other agencies, or private entities, such as social media platforms. This information may be regarding potential criminal activity, such as the threat of potential violence. Other agencies, such as Capitol Police and Park Police obtain threat information from performing their own searches or receiving information from other agencies.

Agencies also have different processes for assessing the credibility of threats based on their intelligence gathering or law enforcement missions. Agencies may review threat-related information to determine whether the information warrants additional action based on factors such as the importance of the target of the threat, the credibility of the threat, and the analysis of the threat. For example, agencies may determine that a tip is a statement protected by the First Amendment (e.g. an individual states they plan to engage in First Amendment demonstration activities), and may not be investigated or assessed further for credibility because of constitutional restrictions.

However, a tip may be identified as outside the scope of First Amendment protected speech, because, for example, it rises to the level of "incitement" (i.e. words meant to inflict injury) or a "true" threat (i.e. the speaker means to communicate a serious expression of an intent to commit an act of unlawful violence).[31] Further, for certain threats, agencies determine whether the threat is credible or actionable by taking steps (i.e. interviewing the individuals making the threat) to determine the intent, plausibility, and imminence of the threat. Agencies may share information on certain threats with law enforcement partners for situational awareness purposes. Agencies may also determine they should take additional actions based on credible threats.

Federal Agencies Identified Threats using Various Sources and Two Found Credible Threats

Federal Agencies Took Steps to Obtain Information and Identify Threats

The 10 agencies in our review each took steps to obtain information regarding January 6, 2021, prior to the attack on the Capitol. Agencies obtained information on potential threats and other details, such as the planned number of participants and demonstration locations. Some agencies took steps to determine whether the threats were "true" or "credible," or shared them with other agencies to determine credibility.[32]

[31]With regards to incitement specifically, the Supreme Court of the United States has said, "the constitutional guarantees of free speech and free press do not permit a State to forbid or proscribe advocacy of the use of force or of law violation except where such advocacy is directed to inciting or producing imminent lawless action and is likely to incite or produce such action." *Brandenburg v. Ohio*, 395 U.S. 444, 447 (1969). To this end, the courts have broken the definition down to a two-prong test, both of which must be satisfied to fall outside the scope of the First Amendment, in which "incitement" is (1) aimed at producing imminent lawless action, and (2) such action is likely to occur. "True threats" are outside the First Amendment because of the interest in "protecting individuals from the fear of violence, from the disruption that fear engenders, and from the possibility that the threatened violence will occur." *R.A.V. v. City of St. Paul, Minn*, 505 U.S. 377, 388 (1992).

[32]For the purpose of this report, we use the term "threat products" to refer to a range of intelligence or information reports and assessments—such as open source intelligence reports, protective intelligence briefs and advisories, and special event assessments—that summarize or assess threat information related to a specific event or events. The FBI refers to these as intelligence reports. We did not define other written communications during and after events (e.g., situation or incident reports, emails) as threat products because agencies did not consider them intelligence reports or assessments.

Figure 4: Capitol Police Photo of January 6, 2021 Attack

Source: U.S. Capitol Police January 6, 2021, photo. | GAO-23-106625

Agencies identified threats through various sources, such as investigations, manual web searches, and other agencies. Threat information indicated groups planning to incite violence at January 6 events, violence between protesters and counterprotesters, and a higher anticipated attendance compared to the prior Make America Great Again (MAGA) I and MAGA II demonstrations.[33] Table 1 describes the sources of information obtained by agencies prior to January 6.

[33]Following the MAGA I demonstrations on November 14, 2020, clashes between protesters and counterprotesters led to one person being stabbed, four police officers being injured, and more than 20 people being arrested for charges including inciting violence, assault, and weapons possession. Following the MAGA II demonstrations on December 12, 2020, clashes between protesters and counterprotesters led to four people being stabbed and more than 30 people being arrested, including six people charged with assaulting officers, four charged with rioting, and one for carrying an illegal electronic shock weapon.

Table 1: Sources of Information Used by Federal Agencies Obtained Prior to the January 6, 2021 Capitol Attack

	Information from arrests or investigations[a]	Information from open sources	Information from other agencies	Information from other sources[b]
Agencies with responsibilities for sharing and addressing domestic threats on January 6				
Federal Bureau of Investigation	Yes	Yes	Yes	Yes
Department of Homeland Security Office of Intelligence & Analysis	Yes	Yes	Yes	No
Capitol Police	Yes	Yes	Yes	Yes
Supporting law enforcement agencies				
Secret Service	Yes	Yes	Yes	Yes
Park Police	Yes	Yes	Yes	Yes
Other supporting agencies				
National Park Service	No	Yes	Yes	Yes
Architect of the Capitol	Yes[c]	Yes	Yes	Yes
House Sergeant at Arms[d]	No	Yes	Yes	No
Senate Sergeant at Arms	Yes	Yes	Yes	Yes
Postal Inspection Service	No	Yes	Yes	No

Source: GAO analysis of agency information. | GAO-23-106625

Note: For the purpose of this report, we refer to all of the federal entities in our scope as federal agencies.

[a]Data from arrests or investigations includes information from an agency's own arrests and investigations as well as information obtained from another agency's arrests and investigations.

[b]For the purposes of this analysis, other sources includes event permit applications, event organizers, and confidential human sources. Other sources excludes information regarding road closures.

[c]The Architect of the Capitol obtained Metropolitan Police Department arrest information from open sources.

[d]The House Sergeant at Arms noted limitations related to reporting on information they obtained and shared pertaining to the events of January 6, due to turnover in staff and leadership and records retention.

State and Local Partners. In addition to the 10 federal agencies, 12 state, local, and regional agencies and organizations played a role in the preparation and response to January 6. Of the 12 agencies we spoke with, six were aware of potential threats prior to the events of January 6, and six learned of them on the day of the attack.[34] State and local agencies played an important role in providing federal agencies with information and coordinating help from other federal, state, and local law enforcement agencies.[35] For example, Capitol Police obtained information from D.C. HSEMA's Fusion Center and Secret Service obtained related information from its Denver Field Office regarding a tip that a member of the Proud Boys had recently obtained ballistic helmets, armored gloves, vests, and purchased weapons, including a sniper rifle and suppressors for the weapons. The tip noted that the individual, along with others, flew to Washington, D.C. on January 5, 2021 to incite violence. As a result, the Deputy Capitol Police Chief requested that Capitol Police issue a Be-on-the-Look-Out alert and attempt to obtain cell phone pings to locate the individual. Secret Service Field Office personnel located and interviewed the individual and his son upon their arrival at the airport. Further, Secret Service Protective Intelligence and Assessment Division personnel took additional steps to review information on social media platforms to identify whether the subjects may have loaded weapons into vehicles used to leave the airport to travel to Washington, D.C.

The D.C. HSEMA Fusion Center also shared information from other agencies, including a Counterterrorism Tip Summary Report developed by the New York State Intelligence Center on December 28, 2020. The report included a social media post in which a user described intent to conduct an attack in Washington, D.C. on January 6—targeting Democratic members of Congress.[36]

---

[34]The state agencies include Maryland Department of Emergency Management, Maryland State Police, and Virginia State Police. The regional agencies include the Metropolitan Washington Council of Governments, the Metropolitan Washington Airport Authority, and the Washington Metropolitan Area Transit Authority. The local agencies include D.C. HSEMA's Fusion Center, MPD, Montgomery County Police Department, Fairfax County Police Department, Prince William County Police Department, and Arlington County Police Department.

[35]A National Fusion Center Association senior official noted there were challenges with sharing threat information between fusion centers leading up to the events of January 6. For example, the official noted that other fusion centers could not share information regarding the criminal history of individuals planning to travel to Washington, D.C. to engage in violence with D.C. HSEMA's Fusion Center, because the information was Law Enforcement Sensitive.

[36]Text contained in the social media post and the related figure were removed from this report because an agency deemed them sensitive.

FBI. In the weeks preceding the January 6 attack on the Capitol, the FBI obtained information across other sources indicating potential threats. Through human source reporting, investigations, and observed activity, the FBI identified the increasing threat of violence at high profile special events, such as the 2020 election and 2021 presidential inauguration.[37] FBI officials we spoke with said that from December 29, 2020 through January 6, 2021, they tracked domestic terrorism subjects that were traveling to Washington, D.C. and developed reports related to January 6 events. As of January 6, 2021, FBI officials noted that the Washington Field Office was tracking 18 domestic terrorism subjects as potential travelers to the D.C. area.

Other information came directly from social media platforms. From October 1, 2020 through January 5, 2021, officials from the FBI we spoke with said they obtained and reviewed 73 potential domestic terrorism-related referrals from one social media platform, and obtained one referral on January 4, 2021 related to potential violence in Washington, D.C. on January 6. In addition, the FBI received information from another social media platform from late November 2020 through January 6, 2021 regarding potential violence at January 6 events. For example, on December 24, 2020, a social media platform emailed information on a user posting threats to kill politicians and to coordinate armed forces of 150,000 individuals on January 6. On January 3, FBI officials said that the FBI Washington Field Office received an online tip from the FBI National Threat Operations Center about a social media user threatening a mass shooting on January 6 in Washington, D.C. This prompted FBI Washington Field Office personnel to look closer at the individual's posts and ultimately determine that the individual did not intend to act on their posts.[38]

DHS I&A. DHS I&A used information from arrests made at prior demonstrations, manual web searches, and other agencies to develop threat products and share information with other agencies. In particular,

---

[37]Agencies may obtain information in various ways, such as information from a confidential human source or from investigative or collection activity. *See generally* Exec. Order No. 12333, § 2.3, 46 Fed. Reg. 59941, 59950 (Dec. 4, 1981) (authorizing collection of information within specified procedures). For example, the FBI considers a confidential human source to be an individual with whom the FBI has established a formal relationship that serves as a source for FBI reporting.

[38]We omitted language identifying specific social media platforms as an agency deemed it sensitive.

DHS I&A officials noted that they identified groups involved in violent stabbings during the MAGA II demonstration. As a result, DHS I&A officials determined street violence could occur on January 6. Moreover, DHS I&A officials developed reports on information they obtained from open sources. For example, DHS I&A collectors obtained posts on January 5, 2021, from a member of the Proud Boys that indicated the individual staked out parking lots of federal building to determine how to bring firearms into D.C. at January 6 events.[39] Further, DHS I&A received information from other agencies. For example, on December 21, 2020, DHS I&A officials received information from D.C. HSEMA Fusion Center officials regarding a threat report that indicated a group threatened to attend demonstrations while armed, with the goal of shooting and killing individuals.

Capitol Police. Capitol Police used information from investigations of individuals planning to attend January 6 events and arrests from prior demonstrations, open sources, and other agencies to develop threat products and share information with other agencies. For example, Capitol Police cited prior arrests of groups that participated in the MAGA I and MAGA II demonstrations. Capitol Police also obtained information from investigations of individuals that planned to engage in criminal activities, such as potential violence during January 6 events. For example, a Capitol Police threat product distributed on January 3, 2021 reported that the subject of an investigation claimed that militia members planned to participate in a demonstration on January 6 while armed.[40] That particular demonstration was in connection with a caravan calling for "patriots" to meet in Washington, D.C. to support the President and participate in the "StopTheSteal" demonstration and the "Wild Protest." Further, the subject of the investigation noted that members were staying in Virginia, and planned to march into Washington, D.C. while armed. Capitol Police Intelligence Operations Section agents worked with local law enforcement on the investigation. Capitol Police also used open sources to develop

[39]DHS I&A's Open Source Collection Operations team is the lead for identifying and reporting threats made online via social media and through other sources of publicly available information. Open Source Collection Operations collectors often conduct their online searches after receiving requests for information or tips about online threats from other DHS I&A offices. They collect threats based on intelligence requirements developed by the Intelligence Community or DHS and provide lead information for law enforcement entities across the country.

[40]D.C. Code provides that, in general, an individual must be licensed to carry a concealed firearm in the District. *See* D.C. Code § 22-4504 et seq.

reports. In particular, a January 4, 2021 report indicated that members of the Proud Boys planned to attend January 6 demonstrations incognito.

Two Federal Agencies Found Credible Threats

From the information obtained, seven of the 10 selected agencies (the FBI, DHS I&A, Capitol Police, Secret Service, Park Police, Senate Sergeant at Arms, and Postal Inspection Service) developed a total of 27 threat products specific to the planned events of January 6 prior to the attack on the Capitol.[41] Of these, 14 products included an assessment of the likelihood that violence could occur. FBI and Capitol Police were the two federal agencies to identify threats that were true or credible.[42] See table 2 for additional information about the assessment of these threats.

[41]We previously reported that federal agencies developed 26 threat products for the events of January 6 based on open sources. In this report, we added an additional report developed by the FBI based on information from a confidential human source.

[42]Agencies have varying definitions of a "true" or "credible" threat. For example, DHS I&A defines a "true threat" as a statement where a subject means to communicate a serious expression of an intent to commit an act of unlawful violence to a particular individual or a group of individuals. The FBI defines a "threat to life" as an imminent or potential threat involving serious bodily injury or significant violent action to anyone, regardless of location to include extraterritorial location. The FBI's Domestic Investigations Operations Guide rules regarding threat to life and information sharing requirements also depend on whether the threat is deemed credible.

Table 2: Selected Federal Agencies Assessed and Identified Credible Threats Prior to the January 6, 2021 Capitol Attack

	Assessed threats for credibility[a]	Reported identifying credible threats[b]
Agencies with responsibilities for sharing and addressing domestic threats on January 6		
Federal Bureau of Investigation	Yes	Yes
Department of Homeland Security Office of Intelligence & Analysis	No[c]	No[c]
Capitol Police	Yes	Yes
Supporting law enforcement agencies		
Secret Service	Yes	No
Park Police	Yes	No
Other supporting agencies		
National Park Service	No	No
Architect of the Capitol	No	No
House Sergeant at Arms	No	No
Senate Sergeant at Arms	No	No
Postal Inspection Service	Yes	No

Source: GAO analysis of agency information. | GAO-23-106625

Note: For the purpose of this report, we refer to all of the federal entities in our scope as federal agencies.

[a]Agencies assessed the credibility of threats either in their own threat products or assessed threats shared by other agencies. The Federal Bureau of Investigation and Department of Homeland Security (DHS) Office of Intelligence and Analysis (I&A) developed intelligence reports that do not include assessments of potential threats. For the purpose of this report, we use the term "threat products" to refer to a range of intelligence or information reports and assessments—such as intelligence information reports, protective intelligence briefs and advisories, and special event assessments—that summarize or assess threat information related to a specific event or events. We did not define other written communications during and after events (e.g., situation or incident reports, emails) as threat products because agencies did not consider them to be intelligence reports or assessments.

[b]Conclusions made by federal agencies regarding information identified in threat products, information obtained on their own (e.g. from manual searches of open sources), or information obtained from other agencies.

[c]DHS I&A did not assess threats for credibility or report that they identified credible threats, because DHS I&A's Open Source Collection Operations team did not share reports on January 6 open source threats with other DHS I&A divisions until after the Capitol attack occurred.

While eight of the 10 agencies in our scope generally reported that they did not identify credible threats for the events of January 6 in their threat products or when assessing information shared by other agencies, the FBI and Capitol Police identified credible threats and took investigative action to address the threats. For example, on January 5, 2021, Capitol Police received a tip regarding plans to block and confront Democratic members of Congress from entering the Capitol through the tunnel system via the basement of the Library of Congress.[43]

Further, Capitol Police personnel identified a group's intentions to form a perimeter around the Capitol complex on the morning of January 6. As a result, Capitol Police deployed a Civil Disturbance Unit platoon one hour earlier than originally planned to increase the security presence at locations identified in the credible threat.

Some Agencies Did Not Fully Process Threat Information or Share Information with Partners

FBI Did Not Consistently Follow Policies for Processing Tips

FBI personnel did not follow policies for processing some tips, resulting in them not being developed into reports that could have been shared with partners. Specifically, the FBI did not process all relevant information related to potential violence on January 6.

According to the FBI's Threat-to-Life Decision Model, the National Threat Operations Center and Field Offices receive tips. FBI's National Threat Operations Center policy establishes controls, specifically noting that, upon receipt of a threat to life tip, an FBI agent is required to document information in a report referred to as a Guardian incident.[44] The Threat Intake Examiner is to share the Guardian with either the appropriate FBI

[43]We have omitted language specifying actions taken and a social media post related to the U.S. Capitol because an agency deemed it sensitive.

[44]A Guardian incident is a report that includes information on a tip provided to the FBI that is then logged into the Guardian system. The FBI determines information may be a "potential threat" after it has been analyzed and determined to be a threat that is outside the scope of First Amendment protection or the Privacy Act, such as a true threat (i.e. the speaker means to communicate a serious expression of an intent to commit an act of violence). The FBI defines a "threat to life" as an imminent or potential threat involving serious bodily injury or significant violent action to anyone regardless of location to include extraterritorial location. Guardians are used to document threats, regardless of their origin, such as analysis of telephone, emails, finances, travel, or records from other agencies. The information is to be shared with the field for determination to open an assessment or predicated investigation.

Field Office or its partner state or local law enforcement agency if appropriate for dissemination.[45] When a Guardian has been assigned to a Field Office, it is managed by an investigative division, such as the Counterterrorism Division. Field Office personnel are to review the tip to ensure it was routed to the appropriate Field Office, immediately conduct investigative checks, and notify their appropriate Supervisory Special Agent of the tip.[46] Field Office personnel also determine whether the Guardian requires additional action, such as opening an investigation or assessment.[47] See figure 5 below regarding steps FBI personnel are to take to process tips.

Figure 5: Steps Federal Bureau of Investigation (FBI) Personnel Take to Process Tips

Source: GAO analysis of FBI information; GAO (clip art). | GAO-23-106625

Note: When the FBI receives a tip from the public about a potential terrorism threat, FBI personnel check to ensure the information meets the "authorized purpose" standard for investigation, under applicable Attorney General Guidelines. If so, then FBI personnel should enter that information into the FBI's Guardian system as a Guardian incident. The Guardian incident is sent to the Field Office for appropriate action. Guardians the FBI has determined have a potential counterterrorism nexus can also be viewed by the FBI's Counterterrorism Division, as the Counterterrorism Division provides oversight on all counterterrorism assessments and investigations. We have omitted certain information from internal policies because an agency deemed it sensitive.

[45]Federal Bureau of Investigation, National Threat Operations Section. FBI personnel are to document tips and share the report with a Supervisory Special Agent to determine if the information meets the requirement for a threat to life designation.

[46]See Field Operations Center Threat-to-Life Incident Reception Guidance.

[47]See Federal Bureau of Investigation, Interim Counterterrorism Policy Implementation Guide Departure (August 14, 2012).

However, the FBI did not process all tips from a social media platform related to January 6 as required by FBI policy. For example:

- **San Antonio Field Office – Austin Residence Agency.** Field Office personnel may obtain and document tips in Guardians to share with FBI divisions, other FBI Field Offices, and Field Office partners. Specifically, Field Office personnel produce reports on information relevant to state, local, and tribal law enforcement partners in their areas of responsibility.[48] Further, Field Office and other FBI personnel must enter all reports of potential or actual terrorist threats and suspected terrorist activity into a database.[49] FBI San Antonio Field Office personnel received tips on counterterrorism threats from Parler but did not develop Guardians or other reports on January 6 events. We reviewed selected posts Parler shared with an agent in the San Antonio Field Office. According to Parler officials, Parler shared posts regarding potential violence at January 6 events with agents located in the FBI San Antonio Field Office from late November 2020 through January 6, 2021. FBI officials confirmed that the FBI San Antonio Field Office obtained 84 emails from Parler from November 20, 2020, through January 20, 2021—45 were related to counterterrorism threats, 26 were related to administrative items or were duplicative, and FBI officials noted that the other 13 emails were not related to counterterrorism threats. FBI officials developed or added information to Guardians based on nine of the 45 emails related to counterterrorism threats, but provided no information on how personnel processed information from the remaining 36 emails. Further, FBI officials noted that the FBI San Antonio Field Office did not develop any related reports on January 6 events as required by policy, such as Guardians, situational information reports, or intelligence information reports but did not indicate why not.[50]

[48]See Federal Bureau of Investigation, Directorate of Intelligence, Intelligence Program Policy Guide 1170PG (October 5, 2021).

[49]See Federal Bureau of Investigation, Interim Counterterrorism Policy Implementation Guide Departure (August 14, 2012).

[50]A "Situational Information Report" is a report that shares raw intelligence information with state, local, and tribal law enforcement partners. FBI Field Office personnel write these reports to share with partners in their area of operation. An "Intelligence Information Report" is a report that shares raw intelligence information outside the FBI to members of the Intelligence Community, law enforcement communities, and FBI Field Offices. Because these report types include a summary of threat information and intelligence, they are included in the scope of our review.

- **Counterterrorism Division.** The FBI's Counterterrorism Division personnel may obtain referrals from liaison partners and are aware of tips documented through a Guardian report by FBI Threat Intake Examiners at the National Threat Operations Center or agents at FBI Field Offices. FBI Counterterrorism Division officials are required to document referrals from liaison partners. FBI Counterterrorism Division officials noted that they obtained tips from the FBI San Antonio Field Office from Facebook and Parler, but they did not develop related reports on information from Parler as required. Specifically, Counterterrorism Division personnel noted that they reviewed 73 potential domestic terrorism related referrals from Facebook from October 1, 2020 through January 5, 2021, and obtained a referral on January 4, 2021, related to potential violence in Washington, D.C. at January 6 events. FBI officials noted that they developed a report on that referral. Moreover, FBI officials noted that the other 72 referrals were not related to potential violence or criminal activity at January 6 events.

  Further, Counterterrorism Division officials noted that they obtained and reviewed information from the FBI San Antonio Field Office from Parler from late November 2020 through January 6, 2021, including information regarding potential violence at January 6 events. FBI officials noted that they did not develop reports as required by policy because most of the information was determined to not be credible. However, FBI policy requires that personnel enter threat-related information into its database, and develop a Guardian once the tip has been assessed for credibility.[51]

The FBI did not ensure personnel consistently followed its policies and procedures for processing information related to potential violence on January 6 it obtained from Parler. If the FBI does not process tips or information according to policy and procedures, information can get lost or may not be developed into threat products that the FBI can share with partners. According to FBI officials, the FBI is in the process of assessing lessons learned and making improvements following the events of January 6. In particular, the FBI is conducting several reviews focusing on challenges the FBI faced in communication, information sharing, and analysis.[52]

[51]See Federal Bureau of Investigation, Interim Counterterrorism Policy Implementation Guide Departure (August 14, 2012).

[52]Due to the ongoing nature of the FBI's after-action review of the processes leading up to January 6, we were not provided documentation of this report.

In line with these efforts, the FBI can benefit from assessing the extent to which, and why, personnel did not process threats shared by social media platforms as required by policy. Such an assessment can help determine if the examples described above are indicative of a larger problem, if existing internal control policies need improvement, or if additional controls are needed. According to *Standards for Internal Control in the Federal Government*, an agency should evaluate control deficiencies identified by ongoing monitoring of the internal control system as well as any separate evaluations.[53] Further, an agency should determine the appropriate corrective actions to remediate the internal control deficiency on a timely basis. Implementing a plan to address any identified deficiencies can help ensure the FBI is processing tips in accordance with policy and increasing awareness of potential threats.

The FBI Shared Threat Information with Partners

The FBI used information from investigations, social media, and other sources to develop threat products and share information with other agencies.

According to *The Attorney General's Guidelines for Domestic FBI Operations,* the FBI has a responsibility to provide information as consistently and fully as possible to agencies with relevant responsibilities to protect the United States and its people from terrorism and other threats to national security.[54] Further, the FBI may share information with federal, state, local, or tribal agencies with law enforcement responsibilities to protect the safety and security of persons and to prevent a crime or threat to national security.

We found that the FBI primarily shared information with its partners, including Capitol Police, in its eGuardian system and via email. Specifically, the FBI shared information on threats to life shared by members of the public, local law enforcement, and FBI headquarter divisions. By January 6, the FBI developed approximately 35 Guardians and assessments regarding unrest related to the election certification—20 of the Guardians were closed and 15 were open.[55] FBI officials noted that

[53]GAO, *Standards for Internal Control in the Federal Government,* GAO-14-704G (Washington, D.C.: September 2014).

[54]*The Attorney General's Guidelines for Domestic FBI Operations* (September 29, 2008).

[55]Guardian reports may be "open" or "closed." These designations refer to that status of the report. Open reports refer to reports that support active or ongoing assessments or investigations, while closed reports have been reviewed and determined to either provide no support to active or ongoing assessments or investigations, or have no nexus to terrorism, cyber, or criminal activity.

Guardians resulted from public reports, referrals of threat information from law enforcement partners, and information from confidential human sources—with the majority of Guardians resulting from social media platforms. The FBI reported sharing information on the Guardians with the appropriate law enforcement partners.

The FBI shared information from Guardians with partners prior to the January 6, 2021, attack. For example, on January 1, 2021, the FBI Washington Field Office shared information with Joint Terrorism Task Force Officers from Capitol Police, Park Police, and Secret Service regarding an open Guardian on a domestic terrorism subject that shared plans to incite violence at January 6 events on TikTok. In addition, on January 3, 2021, the FBI Washington Field Office noted it was tracking four domestic terrorism subjects who planned to travel to the Washington Field Office area of responsibility "for unknown purposes," and shared its findings with the same Task Force Officers. Further, on January 5, 2021, the FBI shared two reports it developed regarding individuals planning to engage in violence against law enforcement and members of Congress with partners, including DHS and Capitol Police.

DHS I&A Did Not Consistently Follow Policies for Processing Potential Threats

DHS I&A identified potential threats based on information they obtained from open source searches and from other agencies.[56] However, DHS I&A personnel did not process some threat information obtained from manual searches and other agencies in threat products as required by policy.

DHS I&A internal controls identify a process for when to obtain, document, and assess threat-related information in reports that are shared with other I&A divisions and partners. According to DHS I&A policy, Open Source Collection Operations team personnel collect publicly available information from open sources, including other

[56]DHS I&A's Open Source Collection Operations team developed two open source intelligence reports prior to the events of January 6 that discussed a potential member of the Proud Boys planning to bring guns to Washington, D.C. and a foreign organization that urged others to "squash elector challenges." DHS I&A also received additional open source threat information from other agencies, such as posts by individuals stating that they plan to shoot and kill counterprotesters.

agencies, to develop reports.[57] Personnel may also develop reports at the request of other DHS I&A divisions, such as the Office of Regional Intelligence. In addition, personnel are to create field intelligence reports from threat information obtained from DHS and other partners when information meets a DHS or intelligence collection requirement, and develop intelligence information reports when information meets an Intelligence Community collection requirement. In addition, DHS I&A policy for developing raw information reports identifies sourcing and citing requirements for open source information.[58] See figure 6 for additional details about the process.

[57]An "open source intelligence report" is a raw report containing information from publicly available sources prior to interpretation or analysis. See I&A Instruction 900 (IA-900): Official Usage of Publicly Available Information. A "field intelligence report" includes raw and unevaluated information of potential intelligence value from a non-DHS department or agency that satisfies certain requirements, such as Homeland Security Information Needs, DHS I&A Priority Intelligence Requirements, or Intelligence Community collection requirements. See I&A Instruction 905 (IA-905): Field Intelligence Report Program. An "intelligence information report" includes raw, unevaluated data from information related to collection requirements or national intelligence requirements. See DHS Instruction 264-01-006 (264-01-006): DHS Intelligence Information Report Standards. These reports do not assess threat information or intelligence, rather the reports summarize such information and are included in the scope of this report.

[58]See I&A Instruction 900 (IA-900): Official Usage of Publicly Available Information. The directive indicates that including the source of information in disseminated products informs a reader's assessment of the quality and the scope of information. Further, sourcing of information enables readers to discover and retrieve information from sources. For posts from open sources, this includes reference to the most original source and includes other elements, such as the date of the post. See James R. Clapper, Director of National Intelligence, Intelligence Community Directive 206 (ICD-206): Sourcing Requirements for Disseminated Analytic Products (January 22, 2015).

Figure 6: Department of Homeland Security (DHS) Office of Intelligence and Analysis (I&A) Steps for Processing Potential Threats Prior to the January 6, 2021 Capitol Attack

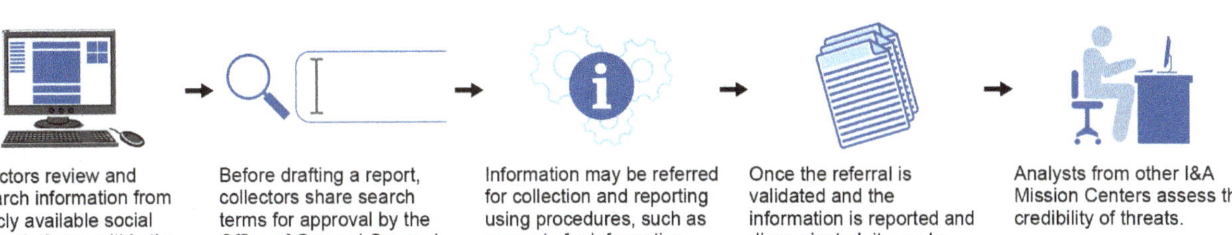

Source: GAO analysis of DHS I&A information; GAO (clip art). | GAO-23-106625

We found, and DHS I&A officials also stated, that DHS I&A personnel did not process some open source threats obtained from manual searches or other agencies in reports. For example,

- **Open Source Collection Operations.** DHS I&A personnel did not develop reports on open source information they obtained regarding potential violence on January 6 prior to the attack, as required by policy. Open Source Collection Operations personnel are required by policy to process open source threat information obtained from manual searches or other agencies in open source intelligence reports.[59] Specifically, DHS I&A officials within the Open Source Collection Operations team obtained open source threat information on threats to law enforcement and potential violence in Washington, D.C., from December 21, 2020 through January 6, 2021. Officials told us they did not develop open source intelligence reports on these potential threats because they determined threats were not credible. However, according to a senior Open Source Collection Operations official, once the threat is documented in an open source intelligence report, DHS I&A divisions other than the Open Source Collection Operations team are to determine whether the threat is credible.
- **Office of Regional Intelligence.** DHS I&A personnel did not develop reports related to January 6 events based on information they obtained from other agencies, as required by policy.[60] Office of Regional Intelligence personnel are to process information obtained

[59]See I&A Instruction 900 (IA-900): Official Usage of Publicly Available Information.

[60]See I&A Instruction 905 (IA-905): Field Intelligence Report Program.

from the field and other agencies in field intelligence reports. For example, Office of Regional Intelligence personnel and other partners, including MPD, received open source threat information from D.C. HSEMA's Fusion Center officials on December 21, 2020. The threat information indicated potential violence at the U.S. Capitol, such as threats to "shoot and kill" counterprotesters and protesters arming themselves to avoid arrest by law enforcement. DHS I&A officials noted that Office of Regional Intelligence personnel did not develop related reports because DHS I&A leadership placed a hold on posting sensitive reports to unclassified systems after a security breach of U.S. government networks, critical infrastructure entities, and private sector organizations.[61] While the steps to safeguard information were warranted, they did not preclude personnel from developing or sharing reports through other means. Such threat information could have been assessed by DHS I&A divisions and documented in reports to be shared with partners to potentially mitigate and address threats.

DHS I&A internal controls did not ensure that personnel followed its policies for processing open source threat information related to the attack on the Capitol on January 6 from manual searches or from other agencies, resulting in threat products not being developed and shared. DHS I&A is implementing changes to its internal control process for reporting related to training and its management structure. Specifically, the DHS Office of Inspector General published a report in March 2022 that also found that DHS I&A obtained open source threat information before January 6, but did not produce any actionable information. The report attributes these actions to inadequate training and not fully considering I&A policy for reporting threat information.[62] In a July 2022 report, the DHS Office of Inspector General similarly cited insufficient policies and procedures to guide staff and inadequate internal controls among other things for the deficiencies related to obtaining, managing, and protecting open source intelligence.[63] In responding to the report, DHS I&A described steps it is taking to improve its intelligence collection

[61]Department of Homeland Security, Office of Inspector General, *I&A Identified Threats prior to January 6, 2021 but Did Not Issue Any Intelligence Products before the U.S. Capitol Breach*, OIG-22-29 (Washington, D.C.: March 4, 2022).

[62]The DHS Office of Inspector General made recommendations to address training of Open Source Collectors. See Department of Homeland Security, Office of Inspector General, *I&A Identified Threats prior to January 6, 2021 but Did Not Issue Any Intelligence Products before the U.S. Capitol Breach*, OIG-22-29 (Washington, D.C.: March 4, 2022).

[63]Department of Homeland Security, Office of Inspector General, *The Office of Intelligence and Analysis Needs to Improve Its Open Source Intelligence Reporting*, OIG-22-50 (Washington, D.C.: July 6, 2022).

and reporting process, including increased training, changing its management structure, and updating policies.

While DHS I&A is implementing internal control changes, I&A has not yet determined whether these changes are effective measures to address internal control deficiencies. As DHS I&A continues with these efforts, it can benefit from assessing the extent to which internal controls are in place to ensure personnel follow existing and updated policies for processing open source threat information. Such an assessment can help DHS I&A further establish a control environment in which there is assurance that policies are followed and enhance the steps DHS I&A is already taking. *Standards for Internal Control in the Federal Government* state that management should remediate identified internal control deficiencies on a timely basis.[64] Taking corrective actions to ensure controls are in place to guide personnel in consistently following policies for processing open source threat information can help provide information to increase DHS I&A and its partners' awareness of potential threats.

DHS I&A Did Not Consistently Share Relevant Threat-related Information with Capitol Police

DHS I&A obtained and identified threat information, but did not ensure the Capitol Police received some information in a timely manner.

According to DHS I&A policy, I&A is responsible for sharing information with operators and decision-makers to identify and mitigate threats to the homeland.[65] Further, DHS I&A policy also states that I&A is committed to delivering timely, actionable, and predictive intelligence to its federal, state, local, and other partners in support of national and homeland security missions.[66]

While DHS I&A developed reports regarding domestic violent extremist activity and potential violence at January 6 events, it did not share all of these reports with Capitol Police.[67] Specifically, DHS I&A developed seven threat products and focused five on the ability for domestic violent

[64]GAO-14-704G.

[65]Office of General Counsel, Department of Homeland Security. Overview of Department of Homeland Security Legal Authorities to Use Social Media. (Washington, D.C.: March 1, 2019).

[66]See I&A Instruction 1000 (IA-1000): Intelligence Oversight Program and Guidelines.

[67]DHS I&A did not share threat products with any partners, including the FBI, Capitol Police, MPD, D.C. HSEMA's Fusion Center, and others, prior to the events of January 6.

extremists to react violently based on election-related issues. DHS I&A shared one product publicly and four products on the Homeland Security Information Network (HSIN) Intelligence (INTEL), which limited access for some organizations.[68] DHS I&A also developed two threat products containing raw threat-related intelligence about potential threats on January 6, but did not share them with Capitol Police. For example, on January 5, 2021, DHS I&A developed an open source intelligence report containing information about threats from a user with enough ammo to "win a small war" who planned to attend January 6 events while armed. However, this report was not shared until January 8, 2021, following the attack.[69] DHS I&A limited the report's distribution to DHS components, the FBI, the Bureau of Alcohol, Tobacco, Firearms and Explosives, and select intelligence agencies. However, DHS I&A officials said they considered sharing the report with Capitol Police, but ultimately did not.

According to DHS I&A officials, they did not share the report with Capitol Police, an agency for whom a report on threats to the U.S. Capitol and surrounding areas would be relevant, because the agency is not within the Intelligence Community, and they believed that Capitol Police was receiving this information from other agencies. DHS I&A officials further said that classification of threat products influenced their decision to distribute them on certain networks, as did their practice of limiting the distribution of information if the product contains information on U.S. persons in conjunction with First Amendment protections and Privacy Act concerns. However, according to Capitol Police officials, they have the ability to receive unclassified and classified intelligence from law

---

[68]HSIN-INTEL is a community of interest located on HSIN. The purpose of HSIN-INTEL is to provide intelligence stakeholders across the Homeland Security Enterprise with a secure platform for sharing of Sensitive But Unclassified (SBU) information, data, products, analytic exchange, and situational awareness. HSIN-INTEL users are federal, state, local, tribal, and territorial intelligence professionals from the homeland security, intelligence, and law enforcement communities. The HSIN-INTEL members include all 15 federal departments and the following National Capital Region partners—D.C. HSEMA's Fusion Center, the Northern Virginia Regional Intelligence Center, Washington/Baltimore High Intensity Drug Trafficking Area, and Regional Information Sharing Systems.

[69]The DHS Office of Inspector General made recommendations to DHS I&A to address timely reviews of open source intelligence reports for upcoming events or urgent threats. To address these recommendations, the DHS I&A Chief Information Officer implemented a new open source intelligence report processing system on August 31, 2021. Further, DHS I&A formalized a policy for producing open source intelligence reports in June 2022, and planned to update existing policies by December 30, 2022. See Department of Homeland Security, Office of Inspector General, *I&A Identified Threats prior to January 6, 2021 but Did Not Issue Any Intelligence Products before the U.S. Capitol Breach*, OIG-22-29 (Washington, D.C.: March 4, 2022).

enforcement and intelligence partners. Further, while DHS I&A may limit certain products to the Intelligence Community, especially if it contains information on U.S. persons, DHS I&A guidance requires it to share information with decision-makers and operators who can help address threats.[70]

The reports that DHS I&A developed addressed information that was relevant to the jurisdictions and protective missions of Capitol Police and other agencies. While DHS I&A is responsible for sharing relevant information with operators and decision-makers to identify and mitigate threats to the homeland, it did not fully do so with regard to Capitol Police in advance of the January 6 events. DHS I&A internal controls did not provide for timely sharing of critical information with the Capitol Police. DHS I&A can benefit from assessing its internal controls related to information sharing to ensure that they allow for effective sharing of threat information. *Standards for Internal Control in the Federal Government* state that management should remediate identified internal control deficiencies on a timely basis.[71] Taking corrective actions to ensure that DHS I&A personnel consistently follow policies for sharing threat-related information can help DHS I&A better achieve its objectives for sharing information about threats and other potential criminal activity with relevant law enforcement agencies, such as Capitol Police, and partners in a timely manner.[72]

---

[70]Based on Executive Order 12,333, DHS I&A personnel may collect, retain, and disseminate information about U.S. persons, and use certain information-gathering techniques, only in accordance with procedures established by the head of the Intelligence Community element concerned or the head of the department, and approved by the Attorney General. See I&A Instruction 1000 (IA-1000): Intelligence Oversight Program and Guidelines. *See also* Exec. Order No. 12333, § 2.3, 46 Fed. Reg. 59941, 59950 (Dec. 4, 1981).

[71]GAO-14-704G.

[72]DHS I&A is currently in the process of responding to multiple recommendations from the DHS Office of Inspector General related to the events of January 6. In particular, the DHS Office of Inspector General recommended that DHS develop and implement policies and procedures on the timely issuance of warning analysis, and implement capabilities for DHS I&A to disseminate intelligence products about threats, among other things. See Department of Homeland Security, Office of Inspector General, *I&A Identified Threats prior to January 6, 2021 but Did Not Issue Any Intelligence Products before the U.S. Capitol Breach*, OIG-22-29 (Washington, D.C.: March 4, 2022).

Capitol Police Did Not Consistently Conduct Supervisory Review of Threat Products

Capitol Police did not include all relevant threat information from other agencies in its threat products developed for January 6. Capitol Police identified potential violence that could occur on January 6 in Washington, D.C. in advance of planned events. However, it did not consistently incorporate complete information into assessments of threats in its threat products, such as information obtained from other agencies regarding an individual traveling to Washington, D.C. to engage in violence at January 6 events.

According to a draft Capitol Police policy in use at the time of the January 6 events, the Intelligence and Interagency Coordination Division is responsible for providing information on demonstrations that have potential impact to agency operations. Personnel must document information on all demonstrations regardless of how the division becomes aware of the information. Further, the policy identifies that Intelligence and Interagency Coordination Division leadership is responsible for ensuring that reports are timely, accurate, and appropriate.[73] In addition, according to the 2021 Capitol Police Board Manual, the Capitol Police is responsible for obtaining, assessing, and sharing threat information with Capitol Police Board agencies.[74] Moreover, *Standards for Internal Control in the Federal Government* state that management should implement control activities through policies, and periodically review policies for continued relevance and effectiveness in achieving the entity's objectives or addressing related risks.[75]

Capitol Police threat products did not contain all relevant information from other agencies. Of the eight threat products developed related to the events of January 6, five were information papers, two were special event

[73]While the draft policy was not finalized prior to the attack, Capitol Police personnel utilized the policy. As of January 2023, the policy was still in draft. See Capitol Police, Intelligence and Interagency Coordination Division, *Standard Operating Procedure: Open Source Guidance for Demonstration Tracking and Communication* (Washington, D.C.: February 2017).

[74]The Capitol Police Board updated the Capitol Police Board Manual of Procedures in December 21, 2021. The language is the same in the 2013 Capitol Police Board Manual of Procedures.

[75]GAO-14-704G.

assessments, and one was an intelligence assessment.[76] Some of these products included the same threat information from other agencies. For example, five threat products included information from DHS and MPD regarding violence and arrests at prior demonstrations and counterprotesters wearing black and throwing projectiles at protesters and law enforcement. However, the products did not include all relevant information Capitol Police had obtained from other agencies, such as a suspicious activity report shared by a D.C. HSEMA Fusion Center official on December 28, 2020. Specifically, the December 28, 2020 report indicated an individual intended to travel to Washington, D.C. and planned to engage in violence during demonstrations on January 6. It is important that the Capitol Police include such information from other sources and agencies in their threat products because it is responsible for disseminating this information to those planning security measures who may not otherwise have access to it. See a photo of the January 6 attack at the U.S. Capitol in figure 7.

[76]"Information papers" are research papers about a particular group, tactics, or other topics that would be of interest to Capitol Police personnel. "Special event assessments" are assessments detailing a major special event at the U.S. Capitol or involving a significant number of members of Congress attending an event, such as the inauguration. "Intelligence assessments" are assessments that contain background information on an event and a threat assessment. Capitol Police considers each additional product as an update of the first threat product. For example, four of five of the information papers are updates that include new information. Both information papers and special event assessments are typically shared with all Capitol Police sworn personnel, select Capitol Police employees (i.e. non-police officers), and personnel from the Architect of the Capitol, and House and Senate Sergeant at Arms. According to Capitol Police officials, intelligence assessments were typically shared with Capitol Police leadership only prior to January 6. These report types are included in the scope of our review because they include either a summary of or assess threat information and intelligence.

Figure 7: Capitol Police Photo of January 6, 2021 Attack

Source: Capitol Police photo above the Capitol Building. | GAO-23-106625

Further, Capitol Police did not update threat product "Bottom Line Up Front" statements—summaries used by Capitol Police to efficiently communicate information including threat assessments—to include threat information contained in threat products. For example, a December 23, 2020 threat product "Bottom Line Up Front" statement noted that Capitol Police expected a number of demonstrations to occur across the U.S. Capitol, White House, and National Mall, but did not indicate that potential violence could occur at these events. Instead, information about potential violence was stated later in the full report, requiring an officer to read the entire report to gather relevant actionable information. Including the most critical information in these statements is important as personnel planning security use them to determine if there might be relevant information in the report.

Capitol Police also did not ensure that relevant threat information carried over to updated products. For example, threat assessments and conclusions in threat products developed after January 3, 2021 did not include a threat previously identified in a January 3, 2021 special event assessment. The specific threat that was omitted indicated that protesters would target Congress rather than counterprotesters.

Without an internal control for reviewing all threat products, critical information and details were left out of threat products. In February 2021, the Capitol Police Inspector General found similar deficiencies in the information that was shared. The Capitol Police Inspector General recommended that Capitol Police update the Standard Operating Procedure to require supervisory review and approval for intelligence products to ensure its products are supported by relevant intelligence information and internally consistent.[77] In response, Capitol Police revised the Standard Operating Procedure.[78] While including updates to the Standard Operating Procedure is a step forward, the revised procedure does not address the need for an internal control requiring that products be reviewed and approved and does not describe the process for doing so.

Because the Capitol Police Inspector General's recommendation addresses the deficiencies we identified and the Capitol Police is taking steps to address it, we are not making an additional recommendation. If implemented, the Inspector General's recommendation to require supervisory review and approval for all threat products can introduce a control environment that will provide better information for decision makers regarding security measures and better position Capitol Police to identify threats of violence.

Capitol Police Did Not Consistently Share Relevant Threat Information Internally

Capitol Police did not internally share relevant threat information agency-wide, resulting in some officers, agents and intelligence staff not having complete information.

Capitol Police policy states that the Intelligence and Interagency Coordination Division Commander is responsible for ensuring

[77]Capitol Police, Office of Inspector General, *Review of the Events Surrounding the January 6, 2021, Takeover of the U.S. Capitol Flash Report: Operational Planning and Intelligence,* Investigative Number 2021-I-0003-A (Washington, D.C.: February 2021).

[78]Capitol Police, *Standard Operating Procedure Analytic Product Sourcing and Standards,* PS-602-08, (Washington, D.C.: August 31, 2021).

coordination and control of intelligence and analysis activities, including obtaining, processing, and sharing of intelligence products in an efficient manner.[79] Moreover, *Standards for Internal Control in the Federal Government* state that management should internally communicate necessary information to achieve the agency's objectives.[80] Further, as part of establishing an organizational structure, management is to consider how units interact in order to fulfill their overall responsibilities. This includes establishing communication lines internally at all levels of the organization that provide methods of communication that can flow down, across, up, and around the organizational structure.

Our review of Capitol Police actions shows that relevant threat information was not shared agency-wide, resulting in some officers not having complete information. Specifically, lower-ranking officers did not receive adequate guidance and warnings about threats of violence on January 6. According to our analysis of survey responses from 315 of 1,782 Capitol Police officers from our prior Capitol attack work, about 129 out of 227 of lower-ranking officers (e.g., private first class) indicated that preoperational guidance was slightly or not at all clear, and 35 of 227 of these officers indicated that no guidance was given to them concerning the use of crowd control tactics.[81] Such information could have been useful to front line officers who were unaware of potential threats for January 6. Our survey of Capitol Police officers further indicated that 190 respondents expressed concerns or made suggestions related to information sharing. Of these respondents, 159 indicated that information, intelligence, and related guidance was not shared with them (either adequately or at all) prior to the January 6 attack.

Selective and limited distribution of threat products also resulted in some officers, agents, and intelligence staff not having complete information. Capitol Police developed eight threat products that indicated potential threats on January 6, but it limited internal distribution of all of these products to senior officials. Capitol Police Intelligence and Interagency

[79]Capitol Police, *Standard Operating Procedure Intelligence Analysis Division Commander Responsibilities*, PS-602-03, (Washington, D.C.: February 1, 2018).

[80]GAO-14-704G.

[81]See GAO-22-104829. Preoperational guidance refers to any communication respondents received from supervisors prior to beginning their duties on January 6. The guidance may have been received the morning of that day or in the days prior to their shift, such as a verbal briefing prior to their shift or emails from management on the planned crowd control tactics for January 6, 2021.

Coordination Division officials began briefing senior personnel ranked at Captain and above following the issuance of a threat product on December 30, 2020. Moreover, the Intelligence and Interagency Coordination Division shared a January 3, 2021 threat product with personnel at the rank of Sergeant and above.[82] Other Capitol Police staff such as sworn officers, agents, and civilian staff assigned to the Intelligence and Interagency Coordination Division were excluded from the distribution of this information that could have been useful in preparing for the events of January 6.

According to Capitol Police officials, they did not share information with some relevant internal stakeholders, in part, because they did not have policies in place for sharing threat-related information across the department. Capitol Police officials said that for every large-scale event, Capitol Police develops an Incident Action Plan that contains the objectives and overall strategy for how the department will manage the event. Capitol Police distributes this document to the cellphone of every officer to help ensure awareness and consistent implementation of the operational plan.

Since the events of January 6, 2021, Capitol Police officials reported taking important steps, including: (1) holding regular briefings for officers and disseminating threat products to front line officers on a routine basis to keep them informed of the current threat environment; and (2) hiring a new director of intelligence who is working with the Assistant Director of Intelligence to implement a number of changes to better deliver intelligence department-wide. While these are positive steps, Capitol Police has not yet established policies for sharing threat-related information across the department. Doing so would be consistent with *Standards for Internal Control in the Federal Government*, which state that management should design control activities to achieve objectives and respond to risks.[83]

Capitol Police has started drafting policies regarding information sharing. However, our review of the draft policy indicates that it would not specify

[82]Higher-ranking officers include lieutenants and sergeants, and lower-ranking officers include private first class.

[83]GAO-14-704G.

at what point front line officers should receive such information.[84] Establishing policies for sharing threat-related information agency-wide can help ensure all relevant personnel have the information they need to perform their duties.

Capitol Police Board Members Shared Limited information with Each Other

The Capitol Police Board did not share all threat-related information with other members of the Board in a consistent and timely manner. We found that the Capitol Police Board member agencies (Capitol Police, House Sergeant at Arms, Senate Sergeant at Arms, and the Architect of the Capitol) generally shared limited threat information among themselves prior to January 6.

According to statute, the Capitol Police Board has oversight of the Capitol Police.[85] Both statute and the 2021 Capitol Police Board Manual of Procedures specify that the role of the Capitol Police Board is to advance coordination between the Capitol Police and the House and Senate Sergeant at Arms.[86] Further, Capitol Police is responsible for briefing entities, including the federal Legislative Branch and the Capitol Police Board, of emerging threats posed by various terrorist groups or individuals. For example, according to the Capitol Police Board Manual, a member of the Capitol Police may provide the Board with an update on security-related information, including but not limited to, intelligence, threats, and dignitary protection schedules.

To meet its threat briefing responsibilities, during the December 16, 2020 briefing to the Capitol Police Board, Capitol Police officials noted that it was monitoring intelligence for the week of January 4, 2021 and that it was monitoring intelligence activity as it relates to groups coming to the Capitol Grounds. According to Capitol Police documentation, they did not convene other Capitol Police Board threat briefings for January 6.

[84]In February 2021, the Capitol Police Office of Inspector General recommended that Capitol Police develop guidance related to coordinating and disseminating intelligence information to all relevant internal entities. Capitol Police, Office of Inspector General, *Review of the Events Surrounding the January 6, 2021, Takeover of the U.S. Capitol Flash Report: Operational Planning and Intelligence,* Investigative Number 2021-I-0003-A (Washington, D.C.: February 2021). As of September 2022 these polices have not yet been finalized. In addition, the Capitol Police Board updated the Capitol Police Board Manual of Procedures on December 21, 2021.

[85]2 U.S.C. § 1901a(a)(1).

[86]*Id.* Capitol Police Board, *Manual of Procedures*, (Washington, D.C.: December 21, 2021).

While the Capitol Police Board Manual specifies that the Capitol Police provides threat briefings to board members, it does not specify roles and responsibilities for members to share threat-related information with each other. We found that Capitol Police Board agencies did not receive complete or timely information from one another. For example, Architect of the Capitol and House and Senate Sergeant at Arms officials told us that they shared information with the Capitol Police, but not with each other. For instance, the Architect of the Capitol obtained information about a threat to the D.C. water system and limited sharing this information to the Capitol Police. Similarly, the Senate Sergeant at Arms developed threat products identifying threats of potential violence by certain groups prior to the events of January 6 but did not share the information with the Architect of the Capitol.

According to officials from Architect of the Capitol and Senate Sergeant at Arms, they did not share information with Capitol Police Board members other than the Capitol Police. For example, the Senate Sergeant at Arms assumed the House Sergeant at Arms received the same threat-related information, because they are in the same meetings and on the same listserv. According to House Sergeant at Arms officials, they did not share information with other Capitol Police Board members because they normally share information directly with the Capitol Police and expect Capitol Police to share that information with the other members of the Board. Additionally, agency officials from the three board members said that they thought it was solely the Capitol Police's responsibility to share information with the Board.

While the Capitol Police Board coordinates to protect the members of Congress, the Capitol building, and the Capitol Complex, according to our analysis, member agencies did not share information with one another before January 6, in part, because its policy does not clarify roles and responsibilities for doing so. Taking steps to ensure Capitol Police Board member agencies share information with one another would be consistent with *Standards for Internal Control in the Federal Government,* which state that management should design control activities to achieve objectives and respond to risks.[87] Updating the Capitol Police Board policy to include specific roles and responsibilities for sharing information can help the Board ensure consistent and timely sharing of threat

[87]GAO-14-704G.

information so that relevant member agencies have information to perform security duties.

Park Police Did Not Process Threat Products to Include Relevant Information

Park Police did not include all relevant threat information from other agencies in its threat products.[88] In particular, Park Police developed seven threat products related to the events of January 6. However, threat products did not include all relevant information obtained from other agencies.

According to Park Police policy, supervisory personnel should familiarize themselves with all content related to special events in the National Capital Region and share that information with officers under their command, as well as relevant law enforcement officers.[89] However, the policy does not clearly state what sources of threat information should be included in the supervisory personnel's review of information. The policy also notes that the Park Police supervisory official onsite may revoke an event permit at any time if continuation of an event presents clear and present danger to the public safety, among other things. Further, National Park Service policy states that the Superintendent may deny permits. According to the policy, the decision to approve or deny a permit must be based on consideration of relevant factors, such as whether the event creates an unsafe environment.[90]

None of the Park Police threat products referred to relevant threat information from other agencies. For example, Park Police products did not include information obtained from the FBI on January 3, 2021 regarding a quick reaction force that planned to bring mace, body armor, head protection, and establish an armed presence outside of Washington, D.C. Further, Park Police did not include all relevant information obtained from manual searches in threat products. For example, four of the threat products referred to general threat information from open sources, such as the potential for violence between protesters and counterprotesters. However, these threat products did not include specific open source

[88]Park Police is within the National Park Service. Both Park Police and National Park Service are within the Department of the Interior.

[89]Park Police General Order (2301): *Demonstrations and Special Events – National Capital Region* (Washington, D.C.: February 23, 2004).

[90]National Park Service Director's Order (53): Special Park Uses. (Washington, D.C.: February 23, 2010).

threat information Park Police obtained related to bombing the White House.

According to Park Police officials, their assessment of potential violence was specific to National Park Service parklands and excluded threats on other property because it was outside of their jurisdiction. For example, Park Police included assessments of threats regarding events at the Ellipse and Lafayette Park, but not assessments of threats to property adjacent to the White House or the White House itself. See figure 8 for an example of open source threat information Park Police obtained from manual searches.

Figure 8: Park Police Obtained a Threat from Twitter Prior to the January 6, 2021 Capitol Attack

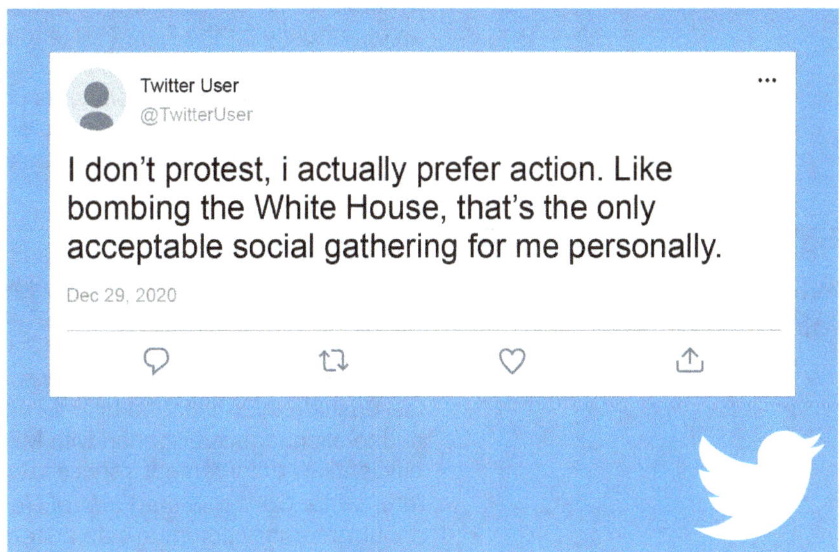

Source: Twitter post obtained by Park Police. | GAO-23-106625

Further, a January 1, 2021 Park Police threat product concluded that there were no threats of violence for January 6 events permitted by the National Park Service.[91] However, the threat product did not include threat information Park Police previously reported. Specifically, the conclusion did not include information related to potential threats Park Police previously identified, such as information from a December 31,

[91]The National Park Service permitted the rally at the Ellipse on January 6, 2021.

2020 threat product that stated that if groups with diametrically opposed beliefs and ideologies come into close contact at events permitted on January 6, violence was almost certain. According to Park Police officials, they did not include this information in their assessment, because such information did not impact Park Police operations.

Park Police did not include information from other agencies in its threat products because its policy does not clearly state the extent to which information related to locations or events outside its jurisdiction should be considered or included in threat products. In August 2021, Park Police officials stated they are in the process of updating guidance on coordination to address assessing and sharing of threat-related information. As of December 2022, Park Police were still in the process of updating the policy. Given what we now know about January 6 and the dynamic threat environment across the National Capital Region, there is an opportunity for the Park Police to clarify its policies to better define the scope of information to consider when developing threat products. As Park Police continues to update its policy, clarifying how it includes and uses information from other agencies pertaining to events and locations outside its jurisdiction can inform operational decisions based on the current threat environment.

Park Police Did Not Share All Relevant Threat Information Internally

While Park Police officials took steps to share information related to January 6, they did not share all relevant threat-related information with the National Park Service ahead of January 6.

Park Police policy requires supervisory Park Police officials to disseminate information to officers under their command at gatherings, and to exchange intelligence with MPD officials to ensure effective and efficient law enforcement services during gatherings.[92] Further, *Standards for Internal Control in the Federal Government* states that management should internally communicate necessary information to achieve the agency's objectives.[93] Further, as part of establishing an organizational structure, management is to consider how units interact in order to fulfill their overall responsibilities. This includes establishing communication lines internally at all levels of the organization that provide methods of

[92]Park Police General Order (2301), *Demonstrations and Special Events- National Capital Region* (Washington D.C.: February 23, 2004).

[93]GAO-14-704G.

communication that can flow down, across, up, and around the organizational structure.

We found that the Park Police did not share all threat products it developed for the events of January 6 with relevant National Park Service permit officials. The Park Police developed seven threat products that included information regarding the potential for violent clashes between protest groups at permitted events. The products also included information about an increasing trend of violent tactics deployed by individuals attending demonstrations with election-based political grievances. While the information in these seven products could have been important in considering whether to grant permits for events on January 6, Park Police shared none of these products with the National Park Service permit official that reviewed the permit for the presidential rally at the Ellipse, and shared two reports with the National Mall and Memorial Park Superintendent.

According to Park Police officials, they did not consistently share threat products with the National Park Service permit officials because distribution of threat products is at the discretion of Park Police commanders and there is no process for determining what it shares. Further, Park Police officials noted that they generally do not share Law Enforcement Sensitive threat products with officials who are not law enforcement personnel or employed within law enforcement agencies. However, they acknowledged that they shared Law Enforcement Sensitive products with the National Park Service previously.

Had Park Police shared relevant threat products with the National Park Service officials reviewing and issuing permits, they may have identified connections between potential threats and January 6 events and responded differently. However, without a process for determining what information is shared, permit officials might not be aware of relevant information that could affect their decisions. Establishing a process to determine what threat-related information Park Police shares with National Park Service permit officials will help ensure permitting decisions consider potential threats.

Most Agencies Used the Same Methods to Identify Threat Information for January 6 and Other Large Demonstrations in D.C.

Nine of the 10 agencies generally used the same methods to identify threats related to potential violence on January 6, 2021, as they did for other large demonstrations in Washington, D.C. Specifically, most agencies identified threats related to other selected large demonstrations—the racial justice demonstrations from late-May to mid-June 2020;[94] the MAGA I demonstrations on November 14, 2020; and MAGA II demonstrations on December 12, 2020—similarly to how they did for January 6, 2021.[95] Table 3 provides summary information about the demonstrations.

Table 3: Information about Other Selected Large Demonstrations in Washington, D.C. and January 6, 2021

D.C. Demonstrations	Dates	Locations	Purpose	Number of attendees	Total number of arrests
Racial justice demonstrations	May 26-June 15, 2020	Lafayette Square, other areas surrounding the White House, downtown	To call for racial justice and police accountability following the death of Mr. George Floyd	Attendance varied each day, reaching a height about 8,000 (estimated)	**431**[a]
Make America Great Again I demonstrations	November 14, 2020	Freedom Plaza, National Mall, U.S. Capitol, Supreme Court	To protest the outcome of the 2020 Presidential election	8,000-10,000 (expected), about 11,000-50,000 (estimated)	**24**[a]
Make America Great Again II demonstrations	December 12, 2020	Freedom Plaza, National Mall, U.S. Capitol, Supreme Court	To protest the outcome of the 2020 Presidential election	About 10,000-20,000 (expected), about 3,000-20,000 (estimated)	**38**[a]

[94]Racial justice demonstrations took place nationwide in the months following the deaths by police of Mr. George Floyd on May 25, 2020 and others. For this review, we are focusing on the racial justice demonstrations that took place in Washington, D.C. from May 26, 2020 through June 15, 2020 as this was the height of the deployment of federal law enforcement agents. We previously reported that at least 12 federal agencies deployed, collectively, up to about 9,300 personnel per day in response to the demonstrations during this time period. For more information about these demonstrations, see appendix III and GAO-22-104470, *Law Enforcement: Federal Agencies Should Improve Reporting and Review of Less-Lethal Force* (Dec. 15, 2021).

[95]We selected the other large demonstrations because they were the closest in time, location, jurisdiction of federal and local law enforcement over the demonstrations, and number of arrests and types of violence compared to the January 6, 2021 Capitol attack.

D.C. Demonstrations	Dates	Locations	Purpose	Number of attendees	Total number of arrests
January 6, 2021 Capitol attack	January 6, 2021	Ellipse, National Mall, U.S. Capitol	To protest the outcome of the 2020 Presidential election	30,000 (expected), At least 35,000 (estimated)	**At least 870[b]**

Source: GAO analysis of agency information (all numerical figures), NBC4 Washington June 5, 2020 report of Metropolitan Police Department data (racial justice demonstrations range), and Los Angeles Times January 5, 2022 report of Department of Defense estimate (January 6, 2021 range). | GAO-23-106625

[a]The D.C. Metropolitan Police Department provided the total number of arrests data for the racial justice and Make America Great Again I and II demonstrations, which includes arrests made during and on the day before and the day after the demonstrations.

[b]This is the total number of arrests reported by the Department of Justice as of September 5, 2022.

For more detailed information about the other large demonstrations, see appendix III.

Based on our analysis, nine of 10 agencies obtained information related to the other large demonstrations similarly to how they obtained information leading up to January 6. For example, the FBI obtained information regarding criminal activity at other large demonstrations from manual web searches of open sources and conducted authorized open source queries to investigate potential or known criminal activity in the lead up to the events of January 6. Seven of 10 agencies also obtained information about the other large demonstrations from other federal, state, or local agencies, and all 10 agencies obtained information about the potential violence on January 6 from other agencies.

The information agencies received across various sources included information about actual and potential property damage caused during demonstrations, actual or potential violence against law enforcement, the potential for extremist groups to commit or incite violence, and actual and potential violence between protesters and counterprotesters, among other information. Figure 9 shows the number of agencies that identified information from each source for each of the other large demonstrations and the potential violence on January 6.

Figure 9: Number of Agencies and their Sources of Information for the Racial Justice, Make America Great Again (MAGA) I, MAGA II Demonstrations and the Potential Violence on January 6, 2021

Number of agencies that identified information[a]

Arrests or investigations[b]

Open sources

Other agencies

Other sources[c]

0 1 2 3 4 5 6 7 8 9 10

Number of agencies

Racial justice demonstrations (May 26—June 15, 2020)

Make America Great Again (MAGA) I demonstrations (November 14, 2020)

MAGA II demonstrations (December 12, 2020)

Potential violence on January 6, 2021

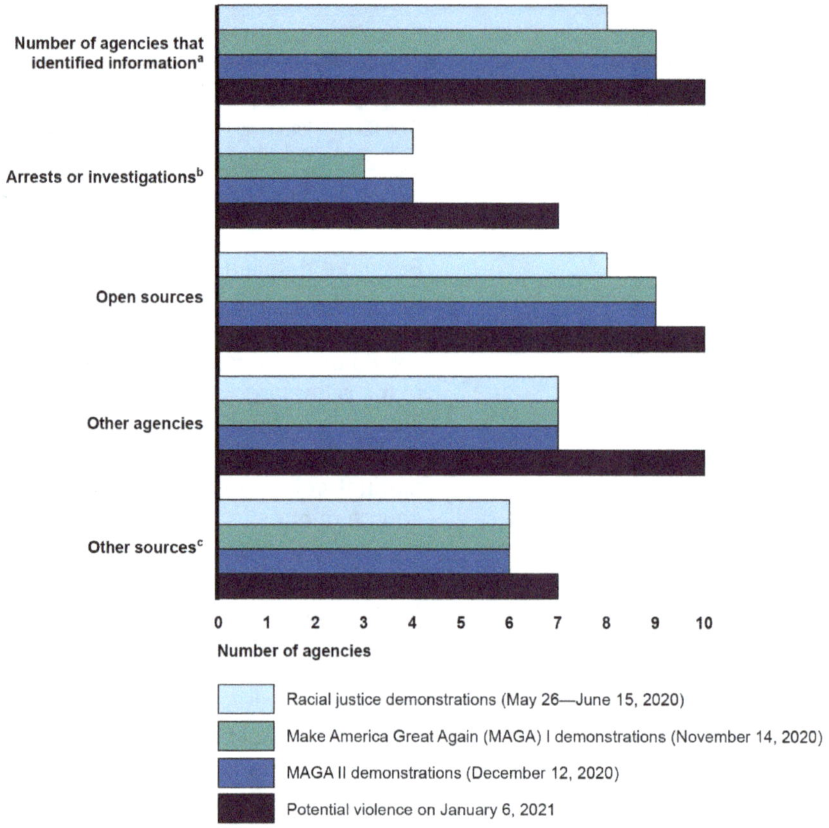

Source: GAO analysis of agency information. | GAO-23-106625

Note: For the purpose of this report, we refer to all of the federal entities in our scope as federal agencies.

[a]According to House Sergeant at Arms officials, the House Sergeant at Arms has no individuals or contracts for individuals whose position description or job duties include open source searches or intelligence gathering, and they did not identify information related to the racial justice or MAGA demonstrations. While monitoring open source data was not part of staffs' official duties, a House Sergeant at Arms official confirmed a few instances in which staff found information from open source data related to January 6 and provided that information to the Capitol Police prior to January 6. The official also stated that the House Sergeant at Arms received a January 3, 2021 Capitol Police threat product about threats related to January 6. The National Park Service also did not obtain information related to the racial justice demonstrations.

[b]This includes information from the agency's own arrests and investigations or other agencies' arrests and investigations. According to Senate Sergeant at Arms officials, the Senate Sergeant at Arms received daily reports from the Capitol Police regarding its arrest information, but the Senate Sergeant at Arms does not engage in investigations or make arrests. The officials stated that Senate Sergeant at Arms may also observe arrest information that is available to the public if posted to open

sources, social media platforms or provided via the media. The Architect of the Capitol obtained Metropolitan Police Department arrest information related to the MAGA II demonstrations from open sources.

[c]For the purposes of this analysis, other sources include event permit applications, event organizers, and confidential human sources. Other sources excludes information regarding road closures. Because of the COVID-19 pandemic, the National Park Service Division of Permits Management did not accept permit applications or issue permits for demonstrations or special activities occurring from approximately March 16- June 22, 2020.

DHS I&A identified information related to the potential violence on January 6 differently than it had for the racial justice and prior MAGA demonstrations. Specifically, after DHS I&A came under scrutiny for compiling intelligence on journalists and non-violent demonstrators in Portland, Oregon in summer 2020, it changed how it identified and reported open source threat information.[96] Within Open Source Collection Operations, 22 of 24 staff told the DHS Office of Inspector General that the scrutiny they received following the summer of 2020 affected their approach to reporting on the potential violence on January 6. According to the DHS Office of the Inspector General, even though collectors reported seeing violent threats related to January 6, they were hesitant to report the information.[97] One collector stated that collectors were afraid to do their jobs because of the fear of being reprimanded by I&A leadership and concerns about congressional scrutiny.[98] DHS has since acknowledged the two events were under different leadership with

[96]For more information about DHS I&A's activities related to the demonstrations in Portland, Oregon, see Department of Homeland Security, *Report on DHS Administrative Review into I&A Open Source Collection and Dissemination Activities During Civil Unrest Portland, Oregon, June through July 2020* (Washington, D.C.: January 6, 2021). See also Department of Homeland Security, Office of Inspector General, *I&A Identified Threats prior to January 6, 2021 but Did Not Issue Any Intelligence Products before the U.S. Capitol Breach*, OIG-22-29 (Washington, D.C.: March 4, 2022).

[97]DHS I&A's Open Source Collection Operations team is the lead for identifying and reporting threats made online via social media and through other sources of publicly available information. Open Source Collection Operations collectors often conduct their online searches after receiving requests for information or tips about online threats from other DHS I&A offices. They collect threats based on intelligence requirements developed by the Intelligence Community or DHS and provide lead information for law enforcement entities across the country.

[98]Department of Homeland Security, Office of Inspector General, *I&A Identified Threats prior to January 6, 2021 but Did Not Issue Any Intelligence Products before the U.S. Capitol Breach*, OIG-22-29 (Washington, D.C.: March 4, 2022).

different thresholds for reporting.[99] Further, the DHS I&A Acting Deputy Under Secretary stated that directions for collectors to report only those threats they were confident were real went too far. Establishing this high level of confidence likely caused collectors to hold back threat information related to January 6.

Seven of 10 agencies used the information they obtained to develop threat products related to the racial justice, MAGA I and MAGA II demonstrations or the potential violence on January 6, 2021.[100] The number and types of threat products developed for the racial justice demonstrations and the MAGA I and II demonstrations and the potential violence on January 6, 2021 differed because the racial justice demonstrations included some unique factors compared to the other demonstrations. Specifically:

- The racial justice demonstrations were largely spontaneous following the death of Mr. George Floyd, while the other events were planned in advance.
- According to National Park Service officials, the racial justice demonstrations on National Park Service land were not permitted events because National Park Service was not issuing permits for events under Centers for Disease Control and Prevention guidance for COVID-19.[101] The demonstrations were largely held on city streets, which does not require a permit. The other events each included permitted events approved by the National Park Service or Capitol Police to take place on federal grounds.

---

[99]For example, the DHS I&A Acting Deputy Under Secretary stated the prior leadership directed collectors to report on information that had a nexus to violence, regardless of credibility. In contrast, the new leadership had the collectors retrained by oversight officers to focus on identifying threats that could be considered "true threats" or "incitement."

[100]For the purpose of this report, we use the term "threat products" to refer to a range of intelligence or information reports and assessments—such as open source intelligence reports, protective intelligence briefs and advisories, and special event assessments—that summarize or assess threat information related to a specific event or events. The FBI refers to these as intelligence reports. We did not define other written communications during and after events (e.g., situation or incident reports, emails) as threat products because agencies did not consider them to be intelligence reports or assessments. Three of the 10 agencies (National Park Service, Architect of the Capitol, House Sergeant at Arms) do not assess threats and did not develop threat products for these events.

[101]Specifically, according to National Park Service officials, because of the COVID-19 pandemic, the agency did not accept permit applications or issue permits for demonstrations or special activities occurring between approximately March 16, 2020 and June 22, 2020.

- The racial justice demonstrations that occurred in Washington, D.C. unfolded over more than 2 weeks, while the MAGA I and MAGA II planned demonstrations and the potential violence on January 6 each covered 1 day.

The information developed about the racial justice demonstrations was different in that it included daily or frequent situation or incident reports during and after demonstrations, as opposed to the formal threat products that assessed threats in advance of the other demonstrations. For example, the FBI, DHS I&A, Park Police, and Secret Service developed and shared numerous situation or incident reports over multiple days in late May or mid June 2020 that identified specific instances of violence against federal and local law enforcement officers, property damage, and arrests. In contrast, for the MAGA I and II demonstrations and the planned lawful demonstrations on January 6, agencies used information from permit applications, social media, and other sources to develop threat products that identified the groups that planned to attend, estimated crowd sizes, and potential for violence in advance of these 1-day events.

Aside from the frequent situation and incident reports developed for the racial justice demonstrations, agencies developed a higher number of threat products for January 6 than for the other events. Compared to the 27 threat products developed regarding January 6, six and five products were developed for the MAGA I and II demonstrations (the other 1-day events), respectively.[102] Agencies developed about 20 threat products for the racial justice demonstrations that occurred over more than 2 weeks.[103] Appendix IV contains a summary of the threat products agencies developed for each event.

Conclusions

The January 6 Capitol attack raised important questions about whether federal agencies adequately identified, processed, and shared threat information. While the FBI identified and shared threat information, it did not process certain referrals from social media platforms according to policies and procedures and, as a result, it failed to share critical information with all relevant partners. The ongoing FBI review of its

[102]In a previous report, we reported that federal agencies developed 26 threat products for the events of January 6 based on open sources. In this report, we added an additional report that was developed by the FBI based on information from a confidential human source.

[103]The number of threat products developed for the MAGA I, MAGA II, and racial justice demonstrations is comprised of the threat products we were able to review but may not demonstrate an exhaustive list.

actions during the weeks preceding January 6, 2021 has not included an assessment of how it processed information. Assessing this process will help determine if the mistakes we identified are isolated or due to a systemic cause. Taking actions on deficiencies identified by its own assessment can help FBI further establish a control environment in which there is assurance that policies for processing information are followed to increase awareness of potential threats.

Similarly, in some cases, DHS I&A did not follow its policies for processing information and did not share all relevant information with its partners. Assessing the extent to which and why these issues occurred can better position DHS I&A to effectively mitigate and respond to risks in the future. Taking corrective actions on deficiencies identified in its assessment can help ensure controls are in place to guide personnel in consistently following policies for processing threat information to develop and share threat products.

The Capitol Police and Park Police did not process threat products to include all relevant information, which resulted in incomplete assessments and conclusions in the products. Both agencies, in addition to the Capitol Police Board, also did not share all relevant information internally. As agencies continue to uncover lessons learned from the Capitol attack on January 6, 2021, it is important that they establish processes to ensure that failures in communicating and sharing important information with those who need it do not happen again. As such, establishing policies and processes for reviewing threat products for current and complete information will help Capitol Police and Park Police ensure they are providing all relevant threat information to those responsible for planning security measures.

Recommendations for Executive Action

We are making 10 recommendations to multiple agencies:

The Director of the FBI should assess the extent to which and why personnel did not process information related to the events of January 6 according to policy. (Recommendation 1)

The Director of the FBI should, following its assessment, implement a plan to address any internal control deficiencies identified to ensure personnel consistently follow policies for processing information. (Recommendation 2)

The DHS I&A Under Secretary should assess the extent to which its internal controls ensure personnel follow existing and updated policies for processing open source threat information. (Recommendation 3)

The DHS I&A Under Secretary should, following its assessment, implement a plan to address any internal control deficiencies identified to ensure personnel consistently follow the policies for processing open source threat information. (Recommendation 4)

The DHS I&A Under Secretary should assess the extent to which its internal controls ensure personnel consistently follow the policies for sharing threat-related information with relevant agencies such as Capitol Police. (Recommendation 5)

The DHS I&A Under Secretary should, following its assessment, implement a plan to address any internal control deficiencies identified to ensure personnel consistently follow the policies for sharing threat-related information with relevant agencies such as Capitol Police. (Recommendation 6)

The Chief of Capitol Police should establish policies for sharing threat-related information agency-wide. (Recommendation 7)

The Capitol Police Board should update its policy to include specific roles and responsibilities for sharing information to ensure consistent and timely sharing of information amongst the Board. (Recommendation 8)

The Chief of Park Police should update its policies to clarify how it uses information from other agencies on potential threats of violence. (Recommendation 9)

The Chief of Park Police should establish a process for determining what threat-related information it shares with National Park Service permit officials. (Recommendation 10)

Agency Comments and Our Evaluation

We provided a draft of the sensitive version of this report to the Department of Justice (DOJ); the Department of Homeland Security (DHS); U.S. Capitol Police; the Capitol Police Board; Architect of the Capitol; House Sergeant at Arms; Senate Sergeant at Arms; and the Department of the Interior; as well as to the U.S. Postal Inspection Service, the Metropolitan Police Department for the District of Columbia, and the District of Columbia Homeland Security and Emergency Management Agency for their review and comment. We received written comments from four agencies (DOJ, DHS, Capitol Police, and the Department of the Interior) that are reprinted in appendixes V through VIII and summarized below. The Capitol Police Board provided comments in an email, which are summarized below. Each of the agencies concurred with our recommendations and noted planned actions to implement them. DOJ, DHS, Capitol Police, Architect of the Capitol, Senate Sergeant at Arms, and Postal Inspection Service also provided technical comments, which we incorporated as appropriate.

DOJ through a letter from the Federal Bureau of Investigation (FBI), concurred with our recommendations to assess the extent to which personnel did not process information related to January 6, and implement a plan to address any internal control deficiencies identified as a result of the assessment. In its letter, the FBI stated that its goal is always to disrupt and stay ahead of the threat, and it is constantly trying to learn and evaluate what it could have done better or differently, especially regarding the attack on the Capitol. The FBI noted that it looks forward to providing updates on its progress as it works toward addressing the recommendations. We are encouraged by the FBI's response and will evaluate the actions once completed.

DHS concurred with all recommendations, which generally include assessing internal controls and addressing any deficiencies. Regarding the recommendations to assess the extent to which its internal controls ensure personnel follow policies for processing open source threat information and sharing threat-related information with relevant agencies, DHS stated that it recognizes the need for a robust internal controls program and noted that it is gathering data to establish a processes for assessing internal controls. DHS agreed with these recommendations and described steps it plans to take and timeframes for completion of these various steps. Once this process is established, DHS expects to complete the recommended assessments by September 29, 2023. For the recommendations to implement plans to address internal control deficiencies, DHS stated that it will work with stakeholders to develop corrective action plans for all identified deficiencies. Specifically, DHS noted that the corrective action plans will include root cause analysis, remediation milestones with due dates, and follow-up actions to be reported to DHS senior leadership on a quarterly basis. We are encouraged that the corrective action plans will address the causes as well as the deficiencies identified. DHS expects to complete the corrective action plans by December 29, 2023. We agree that these are positive steps and look forward to evaluating DHS's actions when completed.

Capitol Police concurred with our recommendation about establishing policies for sharing threat-related information agency-wide. Capitol Police agreed to address this recommendation and stated that the Department is currently drafting a policy that will provide guidance for sharing threat-related information agency-wide. We agree that developing policies for sharing threat-related information agency-wide will help ensure all relevant personnel have the information they need to perform their duties. We will evaluate Capitol Police's actions and polices once completed.

The Capitol Police Board concurred with our recommendation to update its policy to include specific roles and responsibilities for sharing information to ensure consistent and timely sharing of information amongst the Board. The Capitol Police Board agreed to address this recommendation by reviewing the Board's Manual of Procedures in June 2023. Although we agree a review of the current procedures would be helpful, updating the procedures to include specific roles and responsibilities for sharing threat-related information would fully address this recommendation. We will evaluate the Capitol Police Board's actions once completed.

The Department of the Interior concurred with the two recommendations we made to update Park Police policies to clarify how it uses information from other agencies on potential threats of violence, and establish a process for determining what threat related information it shares with National Park Service permit officials. The Department agreed with these recommendations and stated that the Park Police are already taking steps to address them. For example, the letter noted that Park Police initiated an update to the policies utilized by the Park Police Intelligence and Counterterrorism Branch soon after the events of January 6, 2021. The letter added that the policy is in its final review stages, and expects completion by March 2023. In addition, Park Police committed to producing written guidelines defining the process for sharing threat-related information with National Park Service permit officials. The letter noted that this policy would ensure that the appropriate National Park Service officials are briefed about threats that the Park Police deem credible and actionable. We agree that updating its policies for using information from other agencies, and establishing guidelines for sharing threat-related information with National Park Service permit officials will address our recommendations. We will evaluate the Park Police's actions once they are completed.

We are sending this report to congressional leadership, appropriate committees, and the Chief of the U.S. Capitol Police; Architect of the Capitol; Sergeant at Arms of the United States House of Representatives; Senate Sergeant at Arms and Doorkeeper; the Secretaries of Homeland Security and the Interior; the Attorney General; as well as to the Chief Postal Inspector, the Chief of the Metropolitan Police Department for the District of Columbia, and the Director of the District of Columbia Homeland Security and Emergency Management Agency. In addition, the report is available at no charge on the GAO website at https://www.gao.gov.

If you or your staff have any questions about this report, please contact Triana McNeil at (202) 512-8777 or McNeilT@gao.gov. GAO staff who made key contributions to this report are listed in appendix IX.

Triana McNeil
Director
Homeland Security and Justice

List of Requesters

The Honorable Charles E. Grassley
Ranking Member
Committee on the Budget
United States Senate

The Honorable Gary C. Peters
Chairman
Committee on Homeland Security and Governmental Affairs
United States Senate

The Honorable Amy Klobuchar
Chair
Committee on Rules and Administration
United States Senate

The Honorable Bennie G. Thompson
Ranking Member
Committee on Homeland Security
House of Representatives

The Honorable Bryan Steil
Chairman
The Honorable Joe Morelle
Ranking Member
Committee on House Administration
House of Representatives

The Honorable Jamie Raskin
Ranking Member
Committee on Oversight and Accountability
House of Representatives

The Honorable Michael F. Bennet
United States Senate

The Honorable Jake Auchincloss
House of Representatives

The Honorable Nanette Diaz Barragán
House of Representatives

The Honorable Ami Bera, M.D.
House of Representatives

The Honorable Donald S. Beyer, Jr.
House of Representatives

The Honorable Sanford Bishop
House of Representatives

The Honorable Lisa Blunt Rochester
House of Representatives

The Honorable Suzanne Bonamici
House of Representatives

The Honorable Jamaal Bowman
House of Representatives

The Honorable Salud Carbajal
House of Representatives

The Honorable Tony Cárdenas
House of Representatives

The Honorable André Carson
House of Representatives

The Honorable Sean Casten
House of Representatives

The Honorable David N. Cicilline
House of Representatives

The Honorable Yvette D. Clarke
House of Representatives

The Honorable Steve Cohen
House of Representatives

The Honorable Gerald E. Connolly
House of Representatives

The Honorable Joe Courtney
House of Representatives

The Honorable Angie Craig
House of Representatives

The Honorable Jason Crow
House of Representatives

The Honorable Sharice L. Davids
House of Representatives

The Honorable Danny K. Davis
House of Representatives

The Honorable Madeleine Dean
House of Representatives

The Honorable Diana DeGette
House of Representatives

The Honorable Suzan DelBene
House of Representatives

The Honorable Mark DeSaulnier
House of Representatives

The Honorable Debbie Dingell
House of Representatives

The Honorable Lloyd Doggett
House of Representatives

The Honorable Dwight Evans
House of Representatives

The Honorable Lizzie Fletcher
House of Representatives

The Honorable Bill Foster
House of Representatives

The Honorable Lois Frankel
House of Representatives

The Honorable Ruben Gallego
House of Representatives

The Honorable John Garamendi
House of Representatives

The Honorable Jimmy Gomez
House of Representatives

The Honorable Al Green
House of Representatives

The Honorable Raúl M. Grijalva
House of Representatives

The Honorable Jahana Hayes
House of Representatives

The Honorable Brian Higgins
House of Representatives

The Honorable Chrissy Houlahan
House of Representatives

The Honorable Steny H. Hoyer
House of Representatives

The Honorable Jared Huffman
House of Representatives

The Honorable Sheila Jackson Lee
House of Representatives

The Honorable Sara Jacobs
House of Representatives

The Honorable Pramila Jayapal
House of Representatives

The Honorable Henry C. “Hank” Johnson, Jr.
House of Representatives

The Honorable Ro Khanna
House of Representatives

The Honorable Daniel T. Kildee
House of Representatives

The Honorable Derek Kilmer
House of Representatives

The Honorable Andy Kim
House of Representatives

The Honorable Raja Krishnamoorthi
House of Representatives

The Honorable Ann McLane Kuster
House of Representative

The Honorable Barbara Lee
House of Representatives

The Honorable Ted W. Lieu
House of Representatives

The Honorable Zoe Lofgren
House of Representatives

The Honorable Barry Loudermilk
House of Representatives

The Honorable Stephen F. Lynch
House of Representatives

The Honorable Doris Matsui
House of Representatives

The Honorable James P. McGovern
House of Representatives

The Honorable Grace Meng
House of Representatives

The Honorable Seth Moulton
House of Representatives

The Honorable Grace F. Napolitano
House of Representatives

The Honorable Eleanor Holmes Norton
House of Representatives

The Honorable Frank Pallone, Jr.
House of Representatives

The Honorable Jimmy Panetta
House of Representatives

The Honorable Donald M. Payne, Jr.
House of Representatives

The Honorable Scott H. Peters
House of Representatives

The Honorable Dean Phillips
House of Representatives

The Honorable Stacey E. Plaskett
House of Representatives

The Honorable Katie Porter
House of Representatives

The Honorable Raul Ruiz, M.D.
House of Representatives

The Honorable Linda T. Sánchez
House of Representatives

The Honorable Mary Gay Scanlon
House of Representatives

The Honorable Kim Schrier, M.D.
House of Representatives

The Honorable Terri A. Sewell
House of Representatives

The Honorable Mikie Sherrill
House of Representatives

The Honorable Elissa Slotkin
House of Representatives

The Honorable Darren Soto
House of Representatives

The Honorable Abigail D. Spanberger
House of Representatives

The Honorable Haley Stevens
House of Representatives

The Honorable Mark Takano
House of Representatives

The Honorable Rashida Tlaib
House of Representatives

The Honorable Paul Tonko
House of Representatives

The Honorable Norma J. Torres
House of Representatives

The Honorable David Trone
House of Representatives

The Honorable Lauren Underwood
House of Representatives

The Honorable Nydia Velázquez
House of Representatives

The Honorable Debbie Wasserman Schultz
House of Representatives

The Honorable Bonnie Watson Coleman
House of Representatives

The Honorable Nikema Williams
House of Representatives

The Honorable Frederica S. Wilson
House of Representatives

Appendix I: Prior GAO Work Related to the Capitol Attack on January 6, 2021

We have issued six reports examining the preparation, information and intelligence gathering, coordination, and response related to the January 6 attack.[1] Among other things, our prior reports discussed some aspects of how federal agencies shared and used threat information prior to and on January 6. As a result of our findings, we made 11 recommendations to the Department of Homeland Security (DHS), Capitol Police, and the Capitol Police Board.[2] For example:

- In August 2021, we found that the planned protests at the U.S. Capitol and the joint session of Congress to count the electoral votes were not designated by DHS as a National Special Security Event.[3] DHS did not receive a designation request and the events were not automatically designated events like, for example, the presidential inaugurations. There were indications that these events could have been designated, such as the attendance of the Vice President, national media attention, social media posts, and that additional security may have been needed at the Capitol Complex on January

[1]We have issued six prior reports about the January 6 attack. See GAO, *Capitol Attack: Special Event Designations Could Have Been Requested for January 6, 2021, but Not All DHS Guidance Is Clear*, GAO-21-105255 (Washington, D.C.: Aug. 9, 2021); *Capitol Attack: The Capitol Police Need Clearer Emergency Procedures and a Comprehensive Security Risk Assessment Process*, GAO-22-105001 (Washington, D.C.: Feb. 17, 2022), *Capitol Attack: Additional Actions Needed to Better Prepare Capitol Police Officers for Violent Demonstrations*, GAO-22-104829 (Washington, D.C.: Mar. 7, 2022); and *Capitol Attack: Federal Agencies' Use of Open Source Data and Related Threat Products Prior to January 6, 2021,* GAO-22-105963 (Washington, D.C.: May 2, 2022). We also issued two sensitive reports. See GAO, *Capitol Attack: Federal Agencies' Use of Open Source Data and Related Threat Products Prior to January 6, 2021,* GAO-22-105256SU (Washington, D.C.: Feb. 16, 2022); GAO, *Capitol Attack: Federal Agencies Identified Some Threats, but Did Not Fully Process and Share Information Prior to January 6, 2021*, GAO-23-104793SU (Washington, D.C.: Jan. 31, 2023).

[2]See GAO-21-105255, GAO-22-105001, and GAO-22-104829.

[3]GAO-21-105255. In accordance with the process established by the U.S. Constitution and federal law, following the general election for President and Vice President that occurred on November 3, 2020, officials in all 50 states and the District of Columbia certified the results on or prior to December 8, 2020. Electors in each state then convened to vote for President and Vice President on December 14, 2020, and sent signed certificates of the results to federal officials, including the Vice President of the United States, who, in his capacity as President of the Senate, presides over the counting of electoral votes. *See* U.S. Const. art. II, § 1, cl. 2; U.S. Const. amend. XII; 3 U.S.C. § 7 et seq. The joint session of Congress convened to count the electoral votes and declare the results on January 6, 2021, as outlined in the Twelfth Amendment to the U.S. Constitution and federal law. *See* U.S. Const. amend. XII; 3 U.S.C. § 15.

6.[4] We made two recommendations to DHS to consider whether additional factors are needed to designate National Special Security Events, and to clarify existing policy to ensure all relevant stakeholders know who can request National Special Security Event designations in Washington, D.C. DHS disagreed with our recommendations. As of November 2022, DHS has not taken any action on these recommendations. DHS officials stated that they do not concur with these recommendations and requested that GAO consider these recommendations resolved and closed. We have designated these recommendations as a priority for the agency and maintain that it is important for DHS to implement them. We will continue to follow up and monitor DHS's progress on these recommendations.[5]

- In February 2022, we reported that prior to January 6, 10 selected agencies (the FBI, DHS I&A, Capitol Police, Secret Service, Park Police, National Park Service, Architect of the Capitol, House Sergeant at Arms, Senate Sergeant at Arms, and Postal Inspection Service) were aware of publicly available information about planned events on January 6, and seven were aware of potential violence planned for that day.[6] We did not make any recommendations in this report.
- In February 2022, we also found that the Capitol Police's planning for January 6, 2021, did not reflect the potential for extreme violence aimed at the Capitol and did not include contingencies for support from other agencies.[7] In addition, we found that the Capitol Police's process for assessing and mitigating physical security risks to the Capitol complex is not comprehensive or documented. Further, we found that the Capitol Police Board does not have a process for

[4]DHS has specific designations available for planned special events that bolster security-planning processes and coordination between federal, state, and local entities. For example, these designations enhance coordination of protective anti-terrorism measures and counterterrorism assets, and restrict access. These designations include the National Special Security Event and the Special Event Assessment Rating. These designations were not assigned to the events occurring on January 6, 2021.

[5]GAO, *Priority Open Recommendations: Department of Homeland Security,* GAO-22-105702 (Washington, D.C.: July 15, 2022).

[6]GAO-22-105256SU and GAO-22-105963 (public version).

[7]GAO-22-105001. For example, we found that although the Capitol Police had information protesters could be armed and were planning to target Congress, the Capitol Police's plans focused on a manageable, largely nonviolent protest at the Capitol. The Capitol Police's Office of Inspector General previously recommended that the Capitol Police improve its operational planning.

formally considering or making decisions on the Capitol Police's security recommendations. We made four recommendations to the Capitol Police Board and the Capitol Police, related to finalizing and documenting procedures for obtaining outside assistance in an emergency, addressing security risks, and considering security recommendations. The Capitol Police Board did not take a position on our recommendations. The Capitol Police agreed with our recommendations. As of August 2022, the Capitol Police have begun taking steps to implement our recommendations. The Capitol Police Board has not yet provided information to indicate that it has taken action on the recommendations.

- In March 2022, we reported that over 200 of the 315 Capitol Police officers who responded to our survey indicated that preoperational guidance or guidance provided during the attack was slightly clear, not at all clear, or not provided.[8] Further, 56 respondents expressed that they received conflicting information from senior officials on the nature of the threat or that the Capitol Police underestimated the threat. We made five recommendations for the Capitol Police to better understand officers' comprehension of the department's expectations and policies related to use of force by updating training, providing refresher training, providing more realistic training, and developing an action plan to address officers' concerns. Capitol Police agreed with all five recommendations. As of September 2022, Capitol Police have begun taking actions to address these recommendations, such as by planning to conduct quarterly voluntary use of force discussions and increase the amount of hands-on, practical application training. We will continue to monitor the implementation of these efforts.

[8]GAO-22-104829.

Appendix II: Selected Federal Agencies' Policies for Obtaining, Documenting, Assessing, and Sharing Threat Information

This appendix provides summaries of those federal agencies that have policies for obtaining, documenting, assessing, and sharing threat information as of January 6, 2021. For each of the 10 agencies in our scope, we requested policies and standard operating procedures for information sharing, including open source threat information. We developed summaries for the seven agencies (the FBI, DHS I&A, Capitol Police, Park Police, Secret Service, Senate Sergeant at Arms, and Postal Inspection Service) that had such policies. We removed summaries for three agencies (the FBI, Secret Service, and Senate Sergeant at Arms), because these agencies identified that information as sensitive.

DEPARTMENT OF HOMELAND SECURITY (DHS)

OFFICE OF INTELLIGENCE AND ANALYSIS (I&A)

Within DHS, I&A specializes in sharing intelligence and analysis with operators and decision-makers to identify and mitigate threats to the homeland. I&A's main focus is to equip the Department with the intelligence and information it needs to keep the Homeland safe, secure, and resilient. DHS I&A personnel obtain information on threats to homeland security, including domestic terrorism and critical infrastructure.

Source: Department of Homeland Security. | GAO-23-106625

DHS I&A personnel have a process for obtaining threat-related information and conducting searches consistent with essential information requirements. See a high-level summary of the process below.

Obtain threat-related information from web searches and other agencies based on requirements	DHS I&A personnel decide if information meets requirements for a report.	DHS I&A personnel work with DHS I&A peers and supervisory staff to determine if the threat is credible and finalize the report for dissemination.	DHS I&A supervisory staff determine which agencies receive the report for processing or potential analysis.

Source: GAO analysis of DHS information. | GAO-23-106625

POLICIES FOR OBTAINING THREAT-RELATED INFORMATION

The Homeland Security Act of 2002 authorizes the Under Secretary for Information and Analysis to access, receive, and analyze law enforcement information, intelligence information, and other information. The Under Secretary obtains this information from agencies of the Federal Government, state and local government agencies, and private sector entities, and integrates such information to

a) identify and assess the nature and scope of terrorist threats to the homeland;
b) detect and identify threats of terrorism against the United States; and
c) understand such threats in light of actual and potential vulnerabilities of the homeland.[a]

Intelligence Oversight Program and Guidelines I&A Instruction IA-1000: DHS I&A personnel are authorized to engage in intelligence activities where they have a reasonable belief that the activity supports one or more of the national or departmental missions, including but not limited to, domestic terrorism threats. The instruction defines "reasonable belief" standard as a belief based on facts and circumstances that can be articulated based on experience, training, and knowledge of facts. In addition, DHS I&A will only access or use information on a U.S. person when they have appropriate clearances, access, and a mission requirement. Further, to collect such information, DHS I&A personnel must obtain the information overtly or from publicly available sources in the least intrusive way possible, and in accordance with applicable law and policy.

Official Usage of Publicly Available Information I&A Instruction IA-900: Publicly available information refers to unclassified information that has been published or broadcasted in some manner to the general public, is available to the public by subscription or purchase, could lawfully be seen or heard by a casual observer, is made available at a meeting open to the public, or is obtained by visiting any place or attending any event that is open to the public. Social media refers to websites, applications, and web-based tools that connect users to engage in dialogue, share information and media, collaborate and interact. Social media may take many forms, including but not limited to web-based communities and hosted services, social networking sites, video and photo sharing sites, wikis, blogs, virtual worlds, social bookmarking, and other emerging technologies.

Memorandum for Information Regarding First Amendment Protected Activities: According to the May 2019 DHS memorandum, with respect to information pertaining to the First Amendment, DHS I&A personnel shall not collect, maintain, or use information unless expressly granted consent by an individual, authorized federal statute, or information that is related to a criminal, civil, or administrative activity relating to a law DHS enforces or administers.

Overt Human Intelligence Collection Program I&A Instruction IA-907: According to the instruction, DHS I&A personnel obtain information overtly from observing or receiving information from human sources for raw reports.

[a]Homeland Security Act of 2002, Pub. L. No. 107-296, Tit. 1, § 201, 116 Stat 2135, 2145 (amended by Implementing Recommendations of the 9/11 Commission Act of 2007, Pub. L. No. 110-53, Subtit. D, § 531, 121 Stat. 266, 332 (2007) (codified as 6 U.S.C. § 121)).

POLICIES FOR DOCUMENTING THREAT-RELATED INFORMATION

DHS I&A has policies for documenting threats in reports, including reports that contain raw and unevaluated information and finished intelligence reports that contain analysis.

Office of Intelligence and Analysis Field Intelligence Program I&A Instruction IA-905: Field Intelligence Reports contain raw and unevaluated intelligence that satisfies at least one Homeland Security Standing Information Need or one Priority Intelligence Requirement, but does not satisfy an intelligence-related requirement. Reports may be coordinated with non-DHS sources or other components.

DHS Intelligence Information Report Standards Instruction 264-01-006: Intelligence Information Reports contain raw and unevaluated intelligence that satisfy collection or intelligence requirements. These reports are distributed outside of DHS with the Intelligence Community.

Official Usage of Publicly Available Information I&A Instruction IA-900 and Intelligence Oversight Program and Guidelines IA-1000: Open Source Intelligence Reports contain raw information based on information from a public source. These reports may be developed with other agencies and disseminated outside of DHS.

I&A Joint Production with State and Major Urban Area Fusion Centers I&A Instruction IA-904: Joint seal products are produced with other intelligence agencies, such as the Federal Bureau of Investigation (FBI) or Fusion Centers, and carry the seal of participating partners.

Office of Intelligence and Analysis Production of Finished Intelligence I&A Instruction IA-901: Finished Intelligence products include assessment, judgement, and analytic input of DHS I&A personnel that are disseminated outside of DHS. These reports may be developed with other agencies prior to dissemination. According to DHS I&A, raw information reports, such as the Intelligence Information Reports and Open Source Intelligence Reports are used to support analysis in these products.

POLICIES FOR ASSESSING THREAT-RELATED INFORMATION

Overview of DHS Legal Authorities to Use Social Media: DHS defines a true threat as a statement where a subject means to communicate a serious expression of an intent to commit an act of unlawful violence to a particular individual or group of individuals. Further, "political hyperbole" is not considered a true threat, nor is language that is abusive, among other things.

Intelligence Oversight Program and Guidelines I&A Instruction IA-1000: DHS I&A personnel may obtain information on threats to safety to include information on U.S. persons if it is reasonably believed to be necessary to protect against a clear, imminent threat to safety.

POLICIES FOR SHARING THREAT-RELATED INFORMATION

Intelligence Oversight Program and Guidelines I&A Instruction IA-1000: DHS I&A personnel are permitted to disseminate intelligence or information only to the extent there is reasonable belief that dissemination furthers one or more of the national or departmental missions. Dissemination of information on U.S. persons is subject to additional requirements and restrictions. For example, information may be disseminated if there is reasonable belief that dissemination would assist the recipient in fulfilling one or more of their lawful intelligence, counterterrorism, law enforcement, or other homeland security-related functions.

AGREEMENTS FOR SHARING THREAT-RELATED INFORMATION

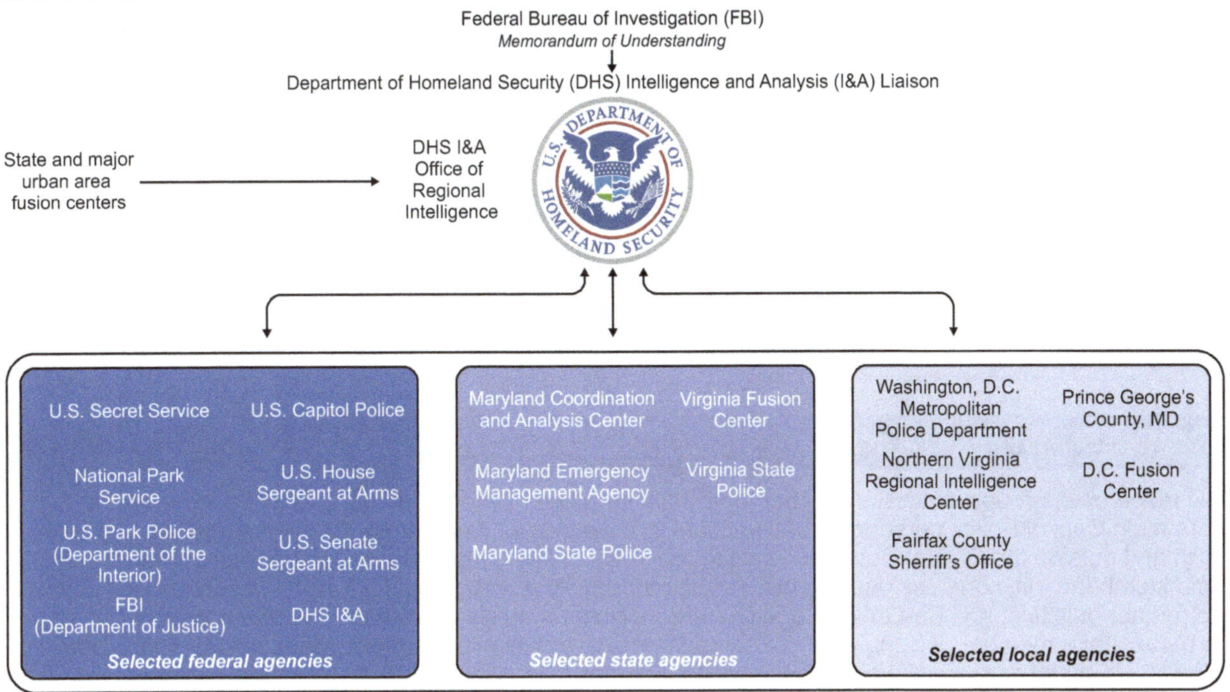

Source: GAO analysis of DHS information. | GAO-23-106625

- **DHS I&A Liaison to the FBI:** On January 3, 2021, DHS I&A leadership asked whether the FBI had information on threats during the week of the electoral vote count. The DHS I&A Liaison noted that the FBI did not determine an anticipated threat level during the FBI Deputy Director's meeting that morning.
- **Fusion Center to DHS I&A Office of Regional Intelligence:** On December 21, 2020, DHS I&A Office of Regional Intelligence received open source information about threats against counter-protesters at unspecified future events in reaction to perceived violence at MAGA II events.
- **Homeland Security Information Network (HSIN):** DHS personnel shared threat products on Communities of Interest within HSIN, and accessed HSIN Situational Awareness Rooms—where other partners, such as U.S. Capitol Police, the U.S. Park Police, and the DHS National Operations Center—posted information on events and updates.

CHANGES TO POLICIES AFTER JANUARY 6, 2021

Following the events of January 6, Secretary Mayorkas announced the creation of a new, dedicated domestic terrorism branch within the Counterterrorism Mission Center in May 2021. The branch is to ensure the Department develops the expertise necessary to combat domestic violent extremism threats by using sound, timely intelligence. In addition, DHS I&A is to continue to utilize the National Network of Fusion Centers and the agency's 120 plus intelligence professionals deployed to collect intelligence in the field.

Based on the findings from the DHS Office of Inspector General on DHS I&A's intelligence activities related to January 6, DHS I&A officials reported that they are updating several policies. In particular, the I&A Chief Information Officer implemented a new Open Source Intelligence Report processing system on August 31, 2021. Further, DHS I&A formalized its policy for producing and disseminating Open Source Intelligence Reports in June 2022, and planned to update IA-900 by December 30, 2022.

U.S. CAPITOL POLICE

INTELLIGENCE AND INTERAGENCY COORDINATION DIVISION (IICD)

The U.S. Capitol Police (Capitol Police) is responsible for safeguarding the Capitol complex, and the Capitol Police IICD, among other divisions, collects and analyzes information to produce intelligence, assess threats, enforce the law, identify risks, and develop and employ risk mitigation. The Capitol Police is responsible for sharing information with the federal legislative branch and the Capitol Police Board on emerging threats by terrorist groups or individuals.

Source: U.S. Capitol Police. | GAO-23-106625

IICD personnel have a process for obtaining threat information and conducting searches related to emerging threats to the Capitol, members of Congress, and their staff and families. See the process below.

Intelligence and Interagency Coordination Division (IICD) personnel obtain information on threats to the Capitol and Congress, including open source data and prior arrests.

IICD develops internal and external reports related to congressional events, permitted events, open source reports, and threat referrals.

IICD personnel consider multiple factors in determining the credibility of threats, such as the plausibility of the threat.

IICD personnel share reports internally and externally based on the scope of the report and the type of threat information contained in the report.

Source: GAO analysis of U.S. Capitol Police information. | GAO-23-106625

POLICIES FOR OBTAINING THREAT-RELATED INFORMATION

IICD researches groups, tactics, and other topics that could be of interest to the Capitol Police. Generally, information Capitol Police personnel obtain relates to the safety of members of Congress when they are within and outside the Capitol Complex. In addition, IICD officers obtain information daily on demonstrations, committee hearings, congressional events, suspicious activity reports, civil disobedience and arrests, internal and partner bulletins, and Be-On-the-Look-Out. IICD officers may also obtain threat-related information at the request of a member of Congress. IICD personnel also obtain information to assess major special events at the U.S. Capitol or events involving a significant number of members, including the Inauguration, State of the Union Address, and Democratic and Republican National Conventions. Within the Capitol Police Special Events Division, Capitol Police personnel obtain information as part of their event permitting process, such as information on the size of the event and prior violence by the event applicant.

Intelligence Priorities Framework: PS-602-11: The framework defines specific collection activities necessary to meet identified priorities for operational activities and priorities for partners that receive analytical products from Capitol Police.

Intelligence Analysis Division Commander Responsibilities: PS-602-03: The Division Commander is responsible for the control of information obtained and in the possession of the Intelligence Analysis Division. Further, the Commander ensures all intelligence is collected efficiently among other responsibilities.

Sourcing Requirements for Analytical Products: PS-602-09: The policy identifies requirements for sourcing information in analytic products disseminated by IICD personnel. The policy defines a source as data that provides material that comprises, contributes to, affects or is used to evaluate, the basis for intelligence analysis. A source can be a person, document, passage, quotation, data record, database, tweet, email, book, web page, or other.

Open Source Guidance for Demonstration Tracking and Communication: CP-1490A: IICD staff members are responsible for actively researching social media and other open sources for information on potential demonstrations in Washington, D.C. and in congressional districts. Further, personnel research demonstration organizers when the demonstration is threatening or otherwise concerning to a member of Congress, the Capitol Complex, or when there is information to suggest that participants may engage in unlawful activity. Personnel obtain information including the date, time, and location of the demonstration, the reason for the demonstration, information on prior civil disobedience and arrests, and background information on the organization leading the demonstration.

POLICIES FOR DOCUMENTING THREAT-RELATED INFORMATION

The Capitol Police has processes for documenting threat-related information in reports that vary by division. For example, IICD developed report templates for different event types and data sources including templates for congressional events, permitted events, open source reports, and threat referrals. Each report template includes information categories, such as background information, social media findings, and adversary threats, among others.

Intelligence Analysis Division Commander Responsibilities: PS-602-03: The Division Commander oversees the timely preparation of intelligence products and ensures all intelligence is processed efficiently.

Sourcing Requirements for Analytical Products: PS-602-09: The policy identifies a variety of analytic products, including disseminated analytic products. Disseminated analytic products contain an assessment, study, estimate, compilation, database, graphic, or interactive publication, based on intelligence research that is reviewed and validated by a supervisor and disseminated outside the Intelligence Analysis Division.

Open Source Guidance for Demonstration Tracking and Communication: CP-1490A: IICD personnel are responsible for logging information regarding a demonstration into a tracker and providing demonstration and situational awareness updates by email.

POLICIES FOR ASSESSING THREAT-RELATED INFORMATION

While the Capitol Police does not have a documented definition of a credible threat, Capitol Police officials noted personnel consider multiple factors in determining the credibility of threat information, including the source, historical information, plausibility of the threat, motivation, degree of corroboration, and other evidence to support the threat. Capitol Police officials noted that they use a definition based on existing case law where a credible threat is subject to legal interpretation, but a threat is any declaration to do harm to a person or property.

Sourcing Requirements for Analytical Products: PS-602-09: Disseminated analytic products contain a source summary statement that explain the quality, credibility, or validity of sources.

POLICIES FOR SHARING THREAT-RELATED INFORMATION

The Capitol Police has processes for sharing reports that include threat information internally and externally. For example, IICD personnel develop Congressional Event Assessments—sharing them internally with its Investigations Division and Dignitary Protection Division and externally with the House and Senate Sergeants at Arms. Further, the Capitol Police has policies for sharing types of threat information externally.

Intelligence Analysis Division Commander Responsibilities: PS-602-03: The Division Commander is responsible for ensuring all intelligence information is disseminated in the most efficient manner possible and approves intelligence for dissemination to external agencies.

Open Source Guidance for Demonstration Tracking and Communication: CP-1490A: Requires IICD personnel to provide demonstration updates to divisions with IICD leadership and personnel with a need-to-know. In addition, demonstration updates are shared across the agency, including to the Capitol Police Command Staff and the Operational Services Bureau.

AGREEMENTS FOR SHARING THREAT-RELATED INFORMATION

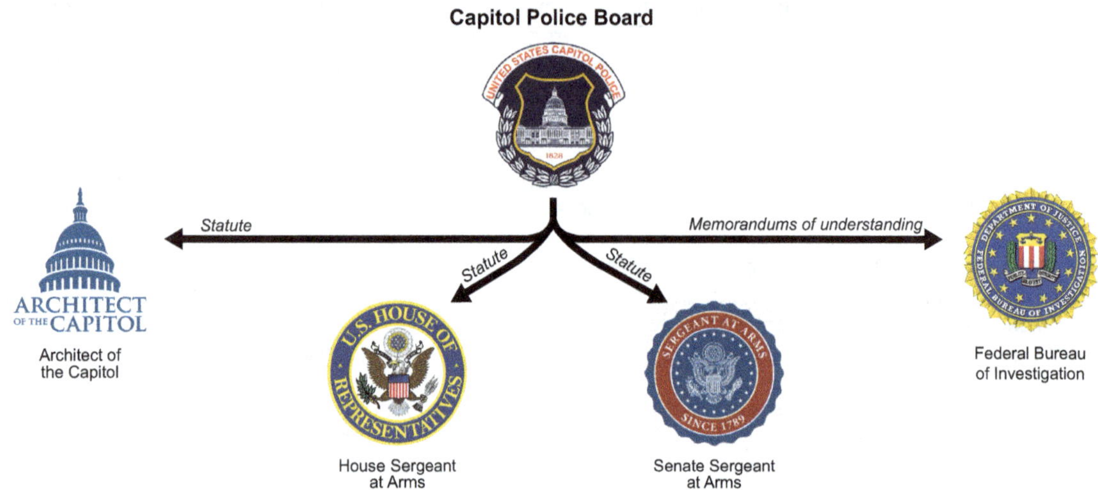

Source: GAO analysis of U.S. Capitol Police information. | GAO-23-106625

- **Sharing with Capitol Police Board Agencies:** As a member of the Capitol Police Board, the Capitol Police is responsible for sharing threat-related information with the federal legislative branch and members of the Board—Architect of the Capitol, House Sergeant at Arms, and Senate Sergeant at Arms. For example, on January 5, 2021, the Capitol Police received information regarding threats to the Capitol tunnels and an airborne threat to the Capitol from the House Sergeant at Arms.

- **Memorandums of Understanding with the FBI:** The Capitol Police has a Task Force Officer with the FBI's National Joint Terrorism Task Force and the Washington Field Office Joint Terrorism Task Force. For example, on January 5, 2021, a Capitol Police Task Force Officer received a situational information report from the FBI Norfolk Field Office regarding threats to Congress.

CHANGES TO POLICIES AFTER JANUARY 6, 2021

Following the events of January 6, IICD updated two policies. In May 2022, IICD updated the Intelligence Priorities Framework to include information categories to guide analytic activities. Categories included information pertaining to individuals or groups seeking to engage in violent acts directed at the U.S. Capitol, members of Congress, or their family members. In August 2021, IICD updated guidelines for analytic product sources. Changes identified that products must be objective, independent, timely, comprehensive, and candid, among other things.

Further, in December 2021, the Police Chief of the Capitol Police, along with other Capitol Police Board members updated the Capitol Police Board Manual to include additional details on Capitol Police briefings to the Board on security issues that may affect Members of Congress. In addition, in March 2021, the Capitol Police issued a new policy on threat assessments that included the definition of a threat—a communication or action showing clear or implied intent to inflict physical, psychological, or other harm. Also, in October 2021, the Capitol Police developed a Critical Incident Response Plan to document coordination of local and federal resources for responding to short-notice and planned events.

DEPARTMENT OF THE INTERIOR

U.S. PARK POLICE

Within the National Park Service, the U.S. Park Police (Park Police) provides law enforcement services to ensure the safety of individuals and to preserve natural and cultural resources. The Park Police may carry out services for events conducted in national parks, such as ensuring that citizens are free to safely exercise their First Amendment rights of free speech and assembly. The Park Police also shares information with the Metropolitan Police Department for the District of Columbia (MPD) on demonstrations that occur within the National Capital Region.

Source: U.S. Park Police. | GAO-23-106625

The Park Police has a process for obtaining threat information about large-scale demonstrations and special events through permitted and non-permitted events. See a high-level summary of the processes below.

U.S. Park Police (Park Police) personnel obtain threat information on permitted and non-permitted events to inform operations and coordination with other law enforcement agencies.

Park Police personnel document threat information on demonstrations in various internal reports for situational awareness purposes.

According to Park Police officials, Park Police has a process for assessing the credibility of threats by determining if an individual has a means, motive, and opportunity to carry out specific threats.

Park Police personnel share threat information on events with D.C. Metropolitan Police Department and other law enforcement agencies during briefings.

Source: GAO analysis of U.S. Park Police information. | GAO-23-106625

POLICIES FOR OBTAINING THREAT-RELATED INFORMATION

The Park Police collects information about large-scale demonstrations to inform security and logistical support, but the agency has limited domestic intelligence capabilities.

36 Code of Federal Regulations (CFR) 7.96: The Park Police may collect information about the plans of organizers of large-scale demonstrations and special events to share with park managers, the MPD, and the Secret Service to assist in the provision of security and logistical support.

General Order 2301: Special Events and Demonstrations in the National Capital Region: The order notes that supervisory Park Police personnel shall familiarize themselves with the content of all applicable special event orders.

According to Park Police officials, Park Police domestic intelligence capabilities are quite limited and involve searching publicly available information. Park Police officials stated that the agency is constantly reviewing information from permits/permittees and open sources for organized events to see whether there are "actionable" threats. For non-permitted events, the Park Police will review open sources and different media outlets and talk to different agencies throughout the area to see what they say about upcoming events.

POLICIES FOR DOCUMENTING THREAT-RELATED INFORMATION

The Park Police does not have policies for documenting threats in reports, but it develops reports for situational awareness purposes. Within the Park Police, the Intelligence and Counterterrorism Branch produces Executive Intelligence Briefings about demonstration activity and Daily Operational Snapshots. Executive Intelligence Briefings list details about events permitted by National Park Service as well as other operational considerations. The snapshots document notable incidents, threat reporting, and scheduled permitted events. Further, Park Police documents demonstrations and events held each month in the Washington Metropolitan Area in a Demonstration and Events Calendar.

POLICIES FOR ASSESSING THREAT-RELATED INFORMATION

The Park Police does not have a policy for assessing threat-related information. According to Park Police officials, the Intelligence and Counterterrorism Branch process for analyzing threat information is similar to the FBI's process, where information is analyzed to determine whether the suspect possesses the means, motive, and opportunity to carry out specific threats.

According to Park Police officials, they make determinations about credible threats based on years of experience reviewing this type of information. For permitted and non-permitted events, the Park Police looks for information within the National Park Service's jurisdiction and whether the information is "actionable." Officials said this involves, for example, distinguishing between whether individuals say they are going to commit a crime, or they are just suggesting that someone should commit the act.

According to Park Police officials, regardless of whether someone is expressing First Amendment-protected views, the Park Police looks for intention to commit a crime or violence, ability, and opportunity. They stated that these three elements—intent, ability, and opportunity—can be applied to a lot of rational thinking. For example, if individuals in a foreign country say they are planning to commit an act of violence in the U.S. at a certain time and place, they may have the intent, but they do not have the ability because they are physically in another country.

POLICIES FOR SHARING THREAT-RELATED INFORMATION

The Park Police is to share information internally, and with MPD, the FBI, and other law enforcement agencies.

General Order 2301: Special Events and Demonstrations in the National Capital Region: Prior to any large public gatherings, including but not limited to demonstrations, picketing, speechmaking, holding of vigils, parades, ceremonies, meetings, and all other forms of public assembly, representatives of Park Police and MPD shall meet to coordinate logistics for the event. Such coordination shall include consideration of the assignment of geographical areas of primary responsibility, exchange of intelligence, data, communications, traffic routing, parking, safety measures, emergency assembly areas, and other necessary arrangements.

Park Police supervisors are to disseminate information about special events internally to officers under their command. The Park Police is to exchange intelligence data externally with MPD, the FBI, and other law enforcement agencies.

AGREEMENTS FOR SHARING THREAT-RELATED INFORMATION

Source: GAO analysis of U.S. Park Police information. | GAO-23-106625

- **Joint Terrorism Task Force:** In a December 28, 2020 Executive Intelligence Brief, Park Police officials indicated that they received an eGuardian report from the FBI regarding plans for individuals to engage in civil disobedience, such as blocking roads leading into D.C.

CHANGES TO POLICIES AFTER JANUARY 6, 2021

As of November 2022, Park Police officials noted that they are in the process of drafting policies related to assessing and sharing threat-related information.

U.S. POSTAL SERVICE

U.S. POSTAL INSPECTION SERVICE

The U.S. Postal Inspection Service (Postal Inspection Service) is the law enforcement arm of the U.S. Postal Service (Postal Service). The Postal Inspection Service enforces laws for using the U.S. mail and ensures the safety of its employees, customers, and facilities through information-gathering activities. Its analysts are assigned proactive intelligence assignments for specific program areas within the organization. The Postal Inspection Service obtains and shares information with external law enforcement partners regarding threats to employees and postal facilities.

Source: U.S. Postal Inspection Service. | GAO-23-106625

Postal Inspection Service personnel have a process for obtaining threat-related information and conducting searches consistent with policy requirements. See a high-level summary of the process below.

U.S. Postal Inspection Service (Postal Inspection Service) personnel obtain information related to the safety of postal employees and facilities.	Postal Inspection Service personnel develop reports on targets and not connected to targets (in cases where they cannot identify the target name).	Postal Inspection Service personnel assess threats based on the totality of the circumstances presented to the investigator.	Postal Inspection Service personnel route reports through peer review and supervisory review before sharing the report with the requesting Inspector and other partners.

Source: GAO analysis of U.S. Postal Inspection Service information. | GAO-23-106625

POLICIES FOR OBTAINING THREAT-RELATED INFORMATION

Postal Inspection Service Handbook AS-353, Guide to Privacy, the Freedom of Information Act, and Records Management: The Privacy Act broadly prohibits the Postal Service from collecting or maintaining records describing or relating to how an individual exercises his or her rights under the First Amendment of the U.S. Constitution. Prohibited records include, among other things, those that describe a person's political, ideological, or religious affiliations and associations. There is an exception to this rule if the Postal Service is expressly authorized by statute to maintain such records, if the individual has expressly authorized the Postal Service to maintain the information, or maintaining the records is pertinent to and within the scope of an authorized law enforcement activity.

Postal Inspection Service Manual 1.1.2.6 Respect for Legal Rights: Activities carried out by Postal Inspection Service personnel must have a valid purpose consistent with the mission of the Postal Inspection Service and must be carried out in conformity with the Constitution and all applicable statutes, executive orders, regulations, and policies. No Postal Inspection Service policies or guidelines authorize investigating or collecting or maintaining information on persons solely for the purpose of monitoring activities protected by the First Amendment or the lawful exercise of other rights secured by the Constitution or laws of the United States.

Standard Operating Procedure—Proactive Intelligence Assignments 2.6: Postal Inspection Service personnel identify a specific target and disseminate supporting information on the target of a proactive intelligence assignment. Personnel obtain two types of intelligence information—1) connected to a target, and 2) not connected to a target. Intelligence connected to a target includes names and monikers used by the target. Intelligence not connected to a target is related to an investigation where the target is not known.

POLICIES FOR DOCUMENTING THREAT-RELATED INFORMATION

Postal Inspection Service has a policy for documenting threats in reports for proactive intelligence assignments. Postal Inspection Service personnel also develop threat assessments through the Cybercrime and Analytics Division.

Standard Operating Procedure—Proactive Intelligence Assignments 2.6: Postal Inspection Service analysts develop intelligence bulletins based on the information they obtain for proactive intelligence assignments. As part of the process for developing such reports, an analyst shares the report with up to two other analysts for peer review. Once the analyst incorporates edits from the peer review, then the report is shared with the Program Manager.

POLICIES FOR ASSESSING THREAT-RELATED INFORMATION

According to Postal Inspection Service officials, they do not have a documented process to determine when a situation poses a credible threat. Officials said that, the Postal Inspection Service is responsible for the security of Postal personnel and assets and is also responsible for investigating a variety of crimes, ranging from robberies and assaults to thefts and fraud. Therefore, what the agency determines constitutes a credible threat is based upon the totality of the circumstances, with Inspectors taking into account all known facts and circumstances of a particular matter. To provide Postal Inspection Service personnel the skills to determine the credibility of a threat they are provided both academy and on-the-job training.

Officials noted that they generally define a "credible threat" as a threat where an individual has the intent and apparent ability to carry out the threat. Postal Inspection Service officials further noted that personnel investigate any statements or actions that cause a reasonable person to be in fear for his or her safety.

POLICIES FOR SHARING THREAT-RELATED INFORMATION

Standard Operating Procedure—Proactive Intelligence Assignments 2.6: When a report developed by the Postal Inspection Service receives approval from the Program Manager, the report is shared with the requesting Inspector.

AGREEMENTS FOR SHARING THREAT-RELATED INFORMATION

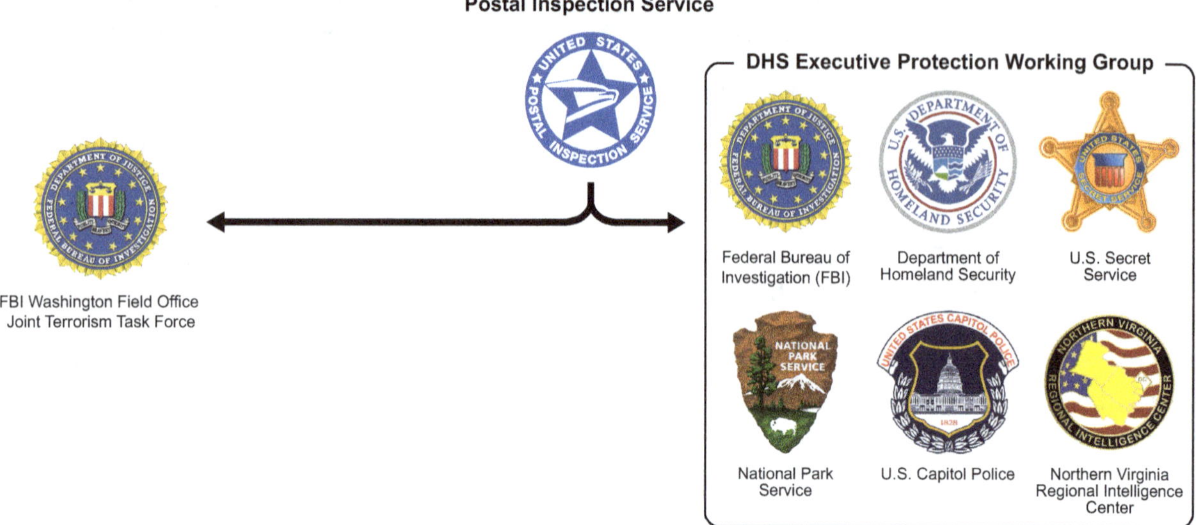

Source: GAO analysis of U.S. Postal Inspection Service information. | GAO-23-106625

- **Joint Terrorism Task Force:** On December 30, 2020, the Postal Inspection Service received information about a tip the Capitol Police received regarding a post from a neo-Nazi-affiliated telegram channel that encouraged supporters to occupy the Capitol on January 6.
- **Department of Homeland Security Executive Protection Working Group:** On December 23, 2020, the Postal Inspection Service shared two threat products with members of the working group. The threat assessments identified potential violence at January 6 events and the inauguration. In particular, one threat assessment indicated that there was a high potential for individuals to incite unrest at the "Million MAGA March."

CHANGES TO POLICIES AFTER JANUARY 6, 2021

Postal Inspection Service officials stated that they revised policies for information-sharing in 2020, before the events of January 6. Changes addressed the review and approval of Postal Inspection Service bulletins before products were shared with external partners.

Appendix III: Summary of Racial Justice and Make America Great Again (MAGA) Demonstrations Prior to January 6, 2021

As discussed in this report, we compared the methods that agencies used to identify and share threat information related to the January 6 demonstrations with those used for other selected large demonstrations in Washington, D.C.—specifically, the racial justice demonstrations from late-May to mid-June 2020;[1] the MAGA I demonstrations on November 14, 2020; and the MAGA II demonstrations on December 12, 2020.[2] This appendix provides more detailed information about these large demonstrations.

Racial justice demonstrations, May 26–June 15, 2020

Nationwide civil unrest and demonstrations occurred following the death of Mr. George Floyd, a 46-year-old African American man, on May 25, 2020, while in police custody in Minneapolis, Minnesota.[3] Related large demonstrations began in Washington, D.C., on May 26, 2020, and continued through mid-June, with smaller, sporadic demonstrations occurring the rest of the summer across the country. While the demonstrations occurred across the city, the main focus of the demonstrations in Washington, D.C. was in the area around the White House and Lafayette Square, which is a federal park located north of the White House (see fig. 10 for map).

[1]Racial justice demonstrations took place nationwide in the months following the deaths by police of unarmed African-Americans, such as Mr. George Floyd on May 25, 2020, and others. For this review, we are focusing on the racial justice demonstrations that took place in Washington, D.C. from May 26, 2020 through June 15, 2020 as this was the height of the deployment of federal law enforcement agents. We previously reported that at least 12 federal agencies deployed, collectively, up to about 9,300 personnel per day in response to the demonstrations during this time period. For more information about these demonstrations, see GAO-22-104470, *Law Enforcement: Federal Agencies Should Improve Reporting and Review of Less-Lethal Force* (Washington, D.C.: Dec. 15, 2021).

[2]We selected these large demonstrations because they were the closest in time, locations, jurisdiction of federal and local law enforcement over the demonstrations, and number of arrests and types of violence compared to the January 6, 2021 demonstrations.

[3]GAO-22-104470, *Law Enforcement: Federal Agencies Should Improve Reporting and Review of Less-Lethal Force* (Washington, D.C.: Dec. 15, 2021).

Figure 10: Map and Image of Demonstrations in Washington, D.C.

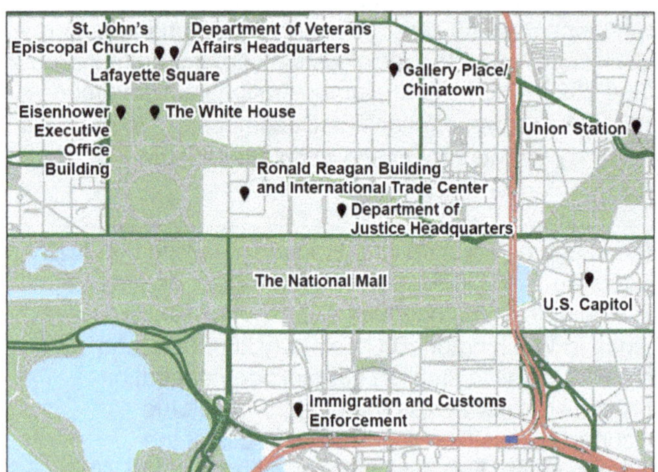

Large demonstration near the Renwick Gallery and Eisenhower Executive Office Building on May 30, 2020

Sources: Department of Homeland Security; MapInfo (map). | GAO-23-106625

Federal Protective Service (FPS) officials estimated that the crowd size of demonstrators had at one time grown to approximately 8,000.[4] The nature of the demonstrations varied, at times being peaceful and violent at other times. Agency officials reported that demonstrators threw dangerous objects at law enforcement, including bricks, rocks, frozen water bottles, and fireworks. For example, FPS, the Secret Service, and the Park Police reported that at least 180 officers were injured during the demonstrations, including concussions, lacerations, exposure to chemical gas, and severe bruising. Damage to structures included broken windows, graffiti on buildings and historic statues, and fires set in vehicles, the Lafayette Square park comfort station (see fig. 11), and the basement of St. John's Church.

[4]FPS is an agency within the Department of Homeland Security (DHS). FPS's responsibility related to demonstrations is to protect federal facilities and safeguard the employees, contractors, and visitors who pass through those facilities every day. FPS can also use a "cross-designation" process to designate additional DHS personnel, pursuant to 40 U.S.C. § 1315(b)(1), to protect federal property.

Figure 11: Images of Property Damage and Dangerous Objects Thrown in Washington, D.C.

Firefighters respond to fire set on comfort station in Lafayette Square in Washington, D.C., on May 31, 2020.

Agency officials reported that demonstrators threw dangerous objects, including fireworks and bricks.

Source: Department of the Interior. | GAO-23-106625

Given the size and nature of the demonstrations, federal agency officials were called in to assist with the protection of federal property, government personnel, and the public. For example, the Secretary of the Interior requested assistance from the District of Columbia National Guard (D.C. National Guard) on May 30, 2020, to provide additional security around the White House and National Mall.[5] Other agencies, such as the Bureau of Prisons, the U.S. Marshals Service, and FPS deployed personnel to Washington, D.C., with the approval of the Attorney General or under a mutual aid agreement.[6] Following the violence during the first few days of the demonstrations, the President requested additional National Guard forces from other states to come to Washington, D.C., to help protect federal functions, persons, and property. On June 1, 2020, the Secretary of Defense requested 5,000 National Guard members to support the D.C. National Guard and law enforcement agencies within the District of Columbia.[7] Appendix IV contains a summary of the threat products agencies developed related to these demonstrations.

Make America Great Again I demonstrations, November 14, 2020

Following the presidential election on November 3, 2020, thousands gathered for a "Million MAGA March" in Washington, D.C. on November 14, 2020 to protest the election outcome and to advocate for the former President and the overall "Make America Great Again" (MAGA) platform. According to a Capitol Police information paper, five demonstrations were planned that day by groups such as Stop the Steal, Women for America First, and others. Some groups gathered at Freedom Plaza in the morning, and several other groups gathered on the National Mall and eventually moved to unite with those gathered at Freedom Plaza. See figure 12 for a Postal Inspection Service map of the rally point and most

[5]National Guard forces who deployed to Washington, D.C., served under Title 32 of the United States Code. 32 U.S.C. §§ 102, 502(f). When operating under this status, National Guard forces are funded by the Department of Defense and are under the command and control of the state Governor or, in the case of D.C., the Secretary of the Army. *See* 32 U.S.C. § 902 (outlining that the Secretary of Defense may provide funds for homeland defense activities).

[6]The Bureau of Prisons (BOP) and U.S. Marshals Service (USMS) are agencies within the Department of Justice. BOP's core responsibilities relate to the incarceration of sentenced prisoners in federal institutions. 18 U.S.C. § 4042(a). However, BOP can also assist other agencies by providing law enforcement officers and assets, when requested. USMS is responsible for protecting the federal judicial process, including protecting individuals in court facilities (such as judges, witnesses, and the visiting public), and managing court security, among other responsibilities. 28 U.S.C. § 566. USMS also has the authority to deputize federal, state, local, or tribal law enforcement officers to perform the functions of a deputy U.S. marshal. 28 C.F.R. § 0.112. Deputized officers have the authority to make arrests under Title 18 of the United States Code. 28 U.S.C. § 566(d).

[7]For more information about the deployment of the National Guard, federal agencies' use of less-lethal force to clear demonstrators from Lafayette Square, and the U.S. National Guard's use of helicopters to clear demonstrators in downtown Washington, D.C., see GAO-22-104470.

likely routes that may have been used by the demonstrators taking part in the "Million MAGA March," or MAGA I demonstrations.

Figure 12: Map of the Million Make America Great Again (MAGA) March rally point and planned routes for the demonstrations

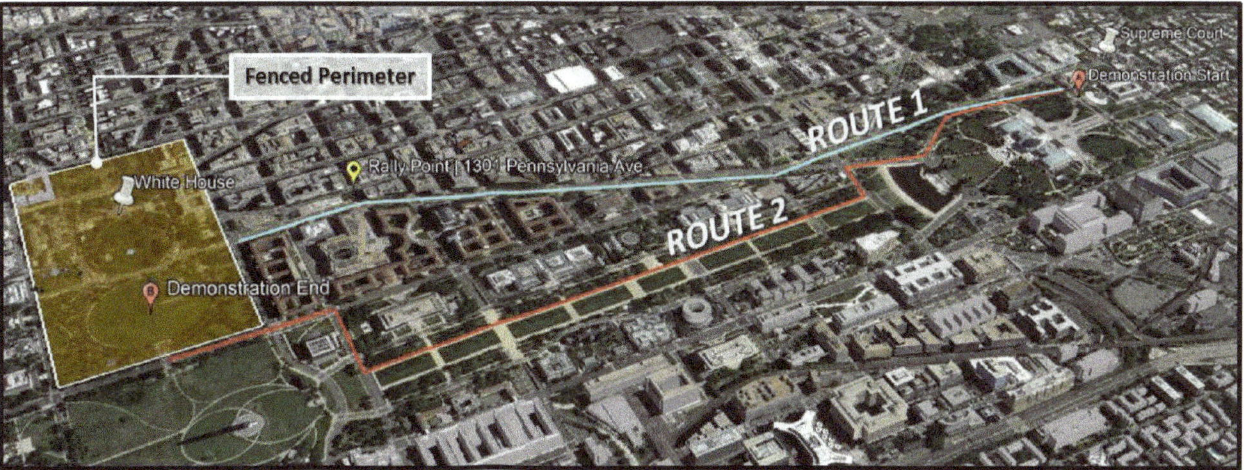

Source: U.S. Postal Inspection Service graphic representation. | GAO-23-106625

According to a Secret Service after-action report, just after 12:00 pm, approximately 11,000 people began marching east on Pennsylvania Avenue towards the U.S. Capitol and Supreme Court. The demonstration continued outside the Supreme Court until approximately 3:15 pm. Once the organized march concluded, the participants fanned out between the Supreme Court and Freedom Plaza. A Capitol Police information paper estimated an attendance in excess of 20,000 participants.

According to a Capitol Police information paper and the Anti-Defamation League, members of several extremist groups, including the Proud Boys, Oath Keepers, and white supremacist groups such as the Groypers, attended the march. Based on social media posts, several agencies also identified that counterprotest groups planned to directly counter the MAGA groups that day. For example, a Park Police intelligence briefing noted that since the election, online tensions had increased between the opposing groups when the groups self-identified as the Proud Boys and The Patriot Front announced they would attend the MAGA rallies to show their support. Figure 13 shows a post identified in a Park Police intelligence briefing.

Figure 13: Instagram post about the Make America Great Again (MAGA) I demonstrations identified in a Park Police intelligence briefing

Instagram User

F*[redacted] MAGA
SAT 14/NOON
1 ST NE AND MARYLAND AVE NE
10 MIN WALK FROM UNION STATION
WEAR BLACK AND WEAR MASK (COVID-19) #F[redacted]MAGA
LOCATION SUBJECT TO CHANGE AS INFORMATION DEVELOPED

Source: Instagram post identified in a U.S. Park Police intelligence briefing. | GAO-23-106625

Four agencies (Capitol Police, Secret Service, Park Police, and Postal Inspection Service) identified the potential for violence or civil disobedience in threat products. For example, according to a Postal Inspection Service situational awareness bulletin, analysts identified multiple posts within the "Stop the Steal" forum of a violent nature to include:

- @user 1: "Antifa and BLM will be there and ready to rumble. The last thing we need are millions of Patriots flooding in unarmed and not ready for a fight. This will be a brawl… I'm a seasoned vet of cracking Antifa and BLM skulls."
- @user 2: "Armed or is that later."
- @user 3: "We are going to have so much fun shutting your [expletive] down."

A Park Police intelligence briefing also noted that all available evidence indicated that a segment within each of the ideologically opposed groups would include members that had used violence in the past to further their cause and there was a high probability of violence if these two groups were allowed to come into direct contact based on past conflicts.[8]

According to the Secret Service after-action report, small groups of counterprotesters appeared at Freedom Plaza and the Supreme Court during the march. They appeared to be loosely organized and there were several instances of confrontations between them and the march participants. Most of the confrontations were verbal, but a couple of physical altercations were reported. After the majority of the Million MAGA March participants had departed the area, several smaller anti-MAGA demonstrations took place beginning at the Black Lives Matter Plaza at 16th and H Street NW.

According to media reports, nighttime clashes between pro-former President protesters, such as the Proud Boys, and counterprotesters at Black Lives Matter Plaza and other downtown locations, became violent. According to one media report, a man in his 20's (whose affiliation was unknown) was stabbed in the back amid the chaos, according to a D.C. fire official, and was transported to the hospital with serious injuries. The D.C. Metropolitan Police Department (MPD) reported 24 arrests, and four officers received non-life-threatening injuries associated with the day's events. The arrests included nine charges for assault; three additional charges for assault on a police officer; six charges for possession of an unregistered firearm or unlawful possession of a firearm, with eight firearms recovered; and four charges for possession of a large capacity ammunition feeding device and unregistered ammunition. Most of the remaining charges were for disorderly conduct or inciting violence.

[8]According to the Park Police intelligence briefing, as an example, a violent confrontation occurred when these groups came into contact on the north slope of the Washington Monument grounds during the July 4, 2020 fireworks show.

Appendix IV contains a summary of the threat products agencies developed prior to these demonstrations.

Make America Great Again II demonstrations, December 12, 2020

Several of the same groups that organized and participated in the MAGA I demonstrations held a second MAGA rally on December 12, 2020 in Washington, D.C. These groups included Women for America First, Stop the Steal, the Proud Boys, and other groups and individuals seeking to demonstrate in support of the former President and to speak out against the 2020 presidential election results. A Secret Service protective intelligence brief noted that December 12, 2020 was 2 days before members of the Electoral College cast their votes for President and Vice President of the United States.[9] According to a Secret Service after-action brief, the MAGA II demonstrations resulted in about 3,000 participants. The demonstrators split between Freedom Plaza, the National Mall, the Capitol and the Supreme Court. Some individuals marching from one place to another, while others protested in one location.

Based on their review of social media posts and observations from the MAGA I demonstrations, five agencies (Capitol Police, Secret Service, Park Police, Senate Sergeant at Arms, and Postal Inspection Service) identified the potential for violence between opposing groups. According to a Capitol Police information paper, the agency estimated fewer crowds for MAGA II compared to MAGA I demonstrations, but they anticipated that the number of Proud Boys for this event would be more than the 200 Proud Boys who attended the demonstrations in November.[10] The paper noted the group's history of violence and social media posts since the MAGA I demonstrations. This prior activity was demonstrative of a growing sentiment among the Proud Boys that they are responsible for

[9]In accordance with the process established by the U.S. Constitution and federal law, following the general election for President and Vice President that occurred on November 3, 2020, officials in all 50 states and the District of Columbia certified the results on or prior to December 8, 2020. Electors in each state then convened to vote for President and Vice President on December 14, 2020, and sent signed certificates of the results to federal officials, including the Vice President of the United States, who, in his capacity as President of the Senate, presides over the counting of electoral votes. *See* U.S. Const. art. II, § 1, cl. 2; U.S. Const. amend. XII; 3 U.S.C. § 7 et seq. The joint session of Congress convened to count the electoral votes and declare the results on January 6, 2021, as outlined in the Twelfth Amendment to the U.S. Constitution and federal law. *See* U.S. Const. amend. XII; 3 U.S.C. § 15.

[10]The Capitol Police information paper identified the Proud Boys as an all-male, far-right extremist group. It stated that the group frequently engages in violence against left-wing protesters and members are required to fight a left-wing protester to attain full membership.

policing areas where they operate which incited violence towards counterprotesters on December 12. In addition, the Secret Service identified that the Proud Boys' Parler and Telegram accounts revealed several comments that called for participants to arrive armed and prepare for violence against left-wing counter-demonstrators.[11]

Further, the Capitol Police information paper noted that in addition to concerns with the Proud Boys' participation in the event and their propensity for violence, there was also some infighting between certain groups. For example, the information paper stated that on November 29, 2020, a member of the Proud Boys posted a statement to his social media account criticizing the Republican Party for supposedly "selling out" its conservative supporters. Figure 14 shows an excerpt of the post.

Figure 14: Excerpt of social media post related to the Make America Great Again (MAGA) II demonstrations identified in a Capitol Police information paper

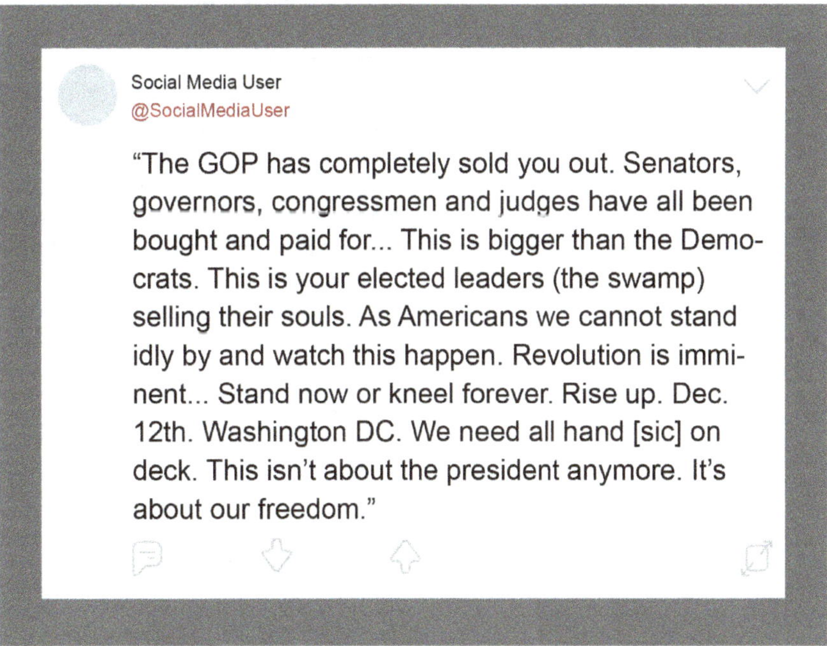

Source: Social media post identified in a U.S. Capitol Police information paper. | GAO-23-106625

[11]We have omitted language and the social media post as an agency deemed it sensitive.

The Capitol Police information paper also stated there were indications that the anti-government organizations, the Oath Keepers and Three Percenters, would also attend the MAGA II demonstrations.[12]

The Capitol Police expected a larger number of counterprotesters than at the MAGA I demonstrations, and several agencies identified the potential for violence between protesters and counterprotesters similar to the MAGA I demonstrations. For example, a Park Police event pre-brief identified that a group of loosely-affiliated local groups planned to counter-protest the permitted demonstrations under the banner of DefendDC.org, and their tactics ranged from non-confrontational and nonviolent tactics to more violent tactics against individuals and property.[13] A Park Police event pre-brief also noted that a more radical group of individuals who self-identify with the Antifa identity and some more extreme local activist groups planned to attend. These individuals were believed to have been the main combatants with the Proud Boys during the November 14 demonstrations.

Following the MAGA II demonstrations, clashes between protesters, counterprotesters, and law enforcement led to four people being stabbed and eight MPD officers sustaining separate injuries. Thirty-eight people were arrested, including 19 people charged with assault, nine more charged with assaulting officers, one with carrying an illegal electronic shock weapon, and others with rioting and inciting violence. According to a Secret Service after-action report, MPD deployed chemical dispersants on several occasions to quell altercations between pro- and anti-former President demonstrators. This occurred mostly in the area north of Black Lives Matter Plaza. In addition, the leader of the Proud Boys burned a

[12]According to the Capitol Police information paper, the Oath Keepers, which claims tens of thousands of present and former law enforcement officials and military veterans as members, is one of the largest radical anti-government groups in the United States today. Three Percenters are part of the militia movement, which supports the idea of a small number of dedicated "patriots" protecting Americans from government tyranny, just as the patriots of the American Revolution protected early Americans from British tyranny. The information paper also noted that because many adherents to the militia movement strongly support the former President, in recent years, Three Percenters have not been as active in opposing the federal government, directing their ire at other perceived foes, including leftists/Antifa, Muslims and immigrants.

[13]The Park Police event pre-brief stated that the groups' objective seemed to be two-fold: to defend Black Lives Matter Plaza and to disrupt the planned demonstration activity of the groups permitted by the National Park Service. It stated that the groups meeting at Black Lives Matter Plaza viewed members of these permitted groups as "fascists" and "white supremacists" and objected to their very presence in their community (in this case, Washington, D.C.).

Black Lives Matter banner torn from a historic African-American church in downtown Washington, D.C. and was later arrested for destruction of property. Appendix IV contains a summary of the threat products agencies developed prior to these demonstrations.

Appendix IV: Federal Agencies' Threat Products Prior to Selected Large Demonstrations in Washington, D.C.

Federal agencies developed several threat products related to the (1) racial justice demonstrations in Washington, D.C. from late-May through mid-June 2020; (2) Make America Great Again (MAGA) I demonstrations in November 2020; (3) MAGA II demonstrations in December 2020; and (4) potential violence on January 6, 2021.[1] The tables below provide additional information about the agencies' threat products for these demonstrations.

Racial Justice Demonstrations Threat Products

From late-May through mid-June 2020, five federal agencies developed threat products related to the racial justice demonstrations that took place in Washington, D.C. immediately following the death of Mr. George Floyd.[2] The agencies developed a total of about 20 threat products based, in part, on open source information.[3] Threat products assessed potential threats for law enforcement planning purposes. The racial justice demonstrations discussed in this review took place over several weeks compared to the other large demonstrations (MAGA I, MAGA II, and January 6 demonstrations) that each took place on a single day. See tables 4 – 7 for additional information about the agencies' threat products.

[1]For the purpose of this report, we use the term "threat products" to refer to a range of intelligence or information reports and assessments—such as open source intelligence reports, protective intelligence briefs and advisories, and special event assessments—that summarize or assess threat information related to a specific event or events. The FBI considers these to be intelligence reports. We did not define other written communications during and after events (e.g., situation or incident reports, emails) as threat products because agencies did not consider them to be intelligence reports or assessments.

[2]As previously stated, racial justice demonstrations took place nationwide in the months following the deaths by police of unarmed African-Americans, such as Mr. George Floyd, on May 25, 2020, and others. For this review, we are focusing on the racial demonstrations that took place in Washington, D.C. from May 26, 2020—the day after Mr. George Floyd's death—through June 15, 2020—the date by which most federal agencies' surge personnel had departed the city. We reviewed agencies' threat products that indicated potential violence could occur in Washington, D.C. or at any lawful racial justice demonstration nationwide, regardless of location (which could include Washington, D.C.), from May 26 through June 15, 2020. Appendix III contains more information about these racial justice demonstrations in Washington, D.C. and the deployment of federal agencies to respond to the protests.

[3]The number of threat products and information in the below table are comprised of the threat products we were able to review but may not demonstrate an exhaustive list.

Table 4: Summary of Threat Products Developed by Selected Federal Agencies Related to the Racial Justice Demonstrations in Washington, D.C. from May 26 through June 15, 2020

Date product developed	Responsible entity	Title and summary of threat product
Federal Bureau of Investigation (FBI)		
June 5, 2020	FBI Washington Field Office	*Situational Information Report: Tradecraft Alert: Identification of Widely-Circulated Image in Social Media Channels Containing Tactical and Force Protection Guidance and Recommended Use of Violent Tactics by Protestors* This report identified that an image showing tactical and force protection guidance for protesters, including the use of violent tactics, had been widely circulated on social media platforms. The image identified roles for protesters, including throwing objects to stop police from advancing.
June 8, 2020	FBI, Department of Homeland Security (DHS), and the National Counterterrorism Center	*Joint Intelligence Bulletin: Domestic Violent Extremists Could Exploit Current Events to Incite or Justify Attacks on Law Enforcement or Civilians Engaged in First Amendment-Protected Activities* This bulletin identified then recent arrests of domestic violent extremists for threats of violence and the potential for increased violent extremist activity occurring during demonstrations taking place across the U.S. in response to the deaths of unarmed African-Americans.
DHS Office of Intelligence and Analysis (I&A)		
May 30, 2020	DHS I&A	*Open Source Intelligence Report: Social media user incites violence to kill more police officers* This report identified that a social media user referenced the May 29, 2020 homicide of a federal law enforcement officer and remarked, "one is not enough," "we need 15 more," and "they [law enforcement] gotta go."
May 30, 2020	DHS I&A	*Open Source Intelligence Report: Social media user posted TTPs [tactics, techniques, and procedures] on how to disable Law Enforcement vehicles* This report noted a social media posting that directed agitators on how to disable law enforcement vehicles.
May 31, 2020	DHS I&A	*Open Source Intelligence Report: Social media video provides TTPs [tactics, techniques, and procedures] on how to interfere with the U.S. National Guard during riots* This report identified that social media postings were emerging that specifically targeted the National Guard and military units. Postings included tactics to inhibit a vehicle operator's visibility and in-depth instructions on how to generally start and operate military vehicles.
May 31, 2020	DHS I&A	*Open Source Intelligence Report: A public encrypted messaging channel administrator incited followers to commit acts of violence toward federal agents* This report cited additional violent threats specifically targeting federal law enforcement officers.
May 31, 2020	DHS I&A	*Open Source Intelligence Report: Encrypted messaging channel administrator posts suggestion for followers to use suppressed subsonic rounds to shoot protesters from wood lines and spread rumors on social media of police officers are shooting protesters* This report identified that at least one other individual is attempting to inspire followers to attack demonstrators and then use online postings to blame these attacks on law enforcement with the goal of causing chaos. It stated that while this individual was not associated with any particular group or cause, the desire to cause generalized chaos and lawlessness is a prime objective of many white nationalist groups.

Date product developed	Responsible entity	Title and summary of threat product
May 31, 2020	DHS I&A	*Open Source Intelligence Report: New York-based anarchist extremist posts inciting threats against U.S. law enforcement* This report stated that a self-identified anarchist extremist made multiple social media postings attempting to inspire others to engage in violent action against law enforcement. Identified posts included "when do we start shooting cops again" and "at what point do we organize to kill them [police]? They [police] don't represent the people."
June 1, 2020	DHS I&A	*Open Source Intelligence Report: Violent extremist social media user posts a 'Riot Guide' containing TTPs [tactics, techniques, and procedures] to be used against police during riots* This report identified that a violent extremist social media user posted a 'Riot Guide' containing tactics, techniques, and procedures to be used against police during riots. The social media user encouraged people "of all creeds" to share the guide.
June 2, 2020	DHS I&A	*Open Source Intelligence Report: Social media user discussed TTPs [tactics, techniques, and procedures] of an anarchist extremist group that staged piles of bricks to incite violence by violent opportunists* This report identified that a social media user claimed that piles of bricks were being staged around the U.S. to fuel violent opportunists in major cities. Source claims that this was a tactic, technique, and procedure being used by Antifa.
June 2, 2020	DHS I&A	*Open Source Intelligence Report: Inglewood, California-based social media user posts multiple threats of violence* This report noted that another social media user promised violence against law enforcement if encountered. The author stated in one post, "at this point if I get pulled over, I'm going to empty both clips and ask no questions. #tired #BLM." Another post stated "... Violence only understands violence, I'm tired of talking [expletive] out and hoping they gone one day understand people who look like me. And don't get me wrong, I'm not a violent dude at all but enough is enough. #BLM #imtired."
June 8, 2020	DHS, FBI, and the National Counterterrorism Center	*Joint Intelligence Bulletin: Domestic Violent Extremists Could Exploit Current Events to Incite or Justify Attacks on Law Enforcement or Civilians Engaged in First Amendment-Protected Activities* This bulletin identified then recent arrests of domestic violent extremists for threats of violence and the potential for increased violent extremist activity occurring during demonstrations taking place across the U.S. in response to the deaths of unarmed African-Americans.
Secret Service		
June 3, 2020	Secret Service Protective Intelligence and Assessment Division (PID)	*Protective Intelligence Brief: Anarchist and Antifa threat to law enforcement* The brief stated that supporters of Antifa may perceive recent demonstrations as an opportunity to carry out criminal acts to further their ideological agenda. Law enforcement and government institutions are likely to be targets of vandalism and critical mass attacks.
June 4, 2020	Secret Service PID	*Protective Intelligence Brief: Threats to Law Enforcement* This brief stated that the targeting of police officers continued to be a persistent threat. For example, right-wing extremist groups, including the Boogaloo Movement, may perceive recent demonstrations as an opportunity to commit criminal acts to further their ideological agenda.
June 6, 2020	Secret Service PID	*Protective Intelligence Advisory: Threats to law enforcement persist after social unrest* This advisory cited examples of attacks on federal, state, and local law enforcement officers involving firearms, incendiary and improvised devices, and vehicle ramming. Such tactics could be used for individual or ambush attacks on law enforcement at any time or place.

Date product developed	Responsible entity	Title and summary of threat product
June 10, 2020	Secret Service PID	*Protective Intelligence Advisory: Continued vigilance needed* This advisory noted recent examples of violence or threats against law enforcement, including a piece of blue tape found on a D.C. Metropolitan Police Department officer's personal vehicle, which may be an attempt to identify and tag the vehicle.
June 17, 2020	Secret Service PID	*Protective Intelligence Advisory: Continued vigilance needed* This advisory noted recent examples of violence or threats against police officers, including that on June 3, 2020, two National Guard soldiers found glass shards in a pizza they had delivered to a Washington, D.C. hotel.
Park Police		
May 31, 2020	Park Police	*Information Note: Projected "Look Ahead" Schedule for Washington Metro Area (WMA) Demonstrations* This note described demonstrations in Washington, D.C. regarding the in-custody death of Mr. George Floyd, which had grown in size and violent behavior by a limited number of individuals. It noted multiple law enforcement and National Guard personnel had been injured during these protests.
June 2, 2020	Park Police	*Information Note: 2 June 2020 Law Enforcement Threat Snapshot* This note provided recent representative threats against federal law enforcement and the National Guard that DHS I&A identified on social media. One post sought to sow chaos, which was noted as a prime objective of many white nationalist groups.
June 4, 2020	Park Police	*Information Note: 4 June 2020 Law Enforcement Threat Snapshot - Civil Unrest* This note provided recent representative acts of violence and threats against law enforcement identified on social media by DHS I&A and by news media, including city police officers being stabbed and shot in what was being described as an unprovoked attack and posts inciting violence.
Senate Sergeant at Arms		
June 1, 2020	Senate Sergeant at Arms Office of Risk and Threat Management	*Open Source Review: Current Protest Environment and Impact on Members* This document summarized open source media attention about the protests and the impact of the protests on the U.S. Senate, such as spray paint found to deface two Capitol Police marked vehicles and a small portion of a Lower West Terrace wall.

Source: GAO analysis of agency information. | GAO-23-106625

Note: For the purpose of this report, we refer to all of the federal entities in our scope as federal agencies. The Senate Sergeant at Arms office performing these activities was previously known as the Open Source Situational Awareness Team and also as the Intelligence and Protective Services.

Make America Great Again (MAGA) I Demonstrations Threat Products

In November 2020, four federal agencies developed at least six threat products related to the MAGA I demonstrations on November 14, 2020.[4] The agencies developed the threat products based, in part, on open source information. Threat products included briefing statements that summarized protest-related information for operational use, and other products that assessed potential threats for law enforcement planning

[4]The number of threat products and information in the below table are comprised of the threat products we were able to review but may not demonstrate an exhaustive list.

purposes. See table 5 for additional information about the agencies' threat products.

Table 5: Summary of Threat Products Developed by Selected Federal Agencies Prior to the Make America Great Again (MAGA) I Demonstrations on November 14, 2020

Date product developed	Responsible entity	Title and summary of threat product
Secret Service		
November 12, 2020	Secret Service Protective Intelligence and Assessment Division (PID)	*Protective Intelligence Brief: Million MAGA March* This brief provided information about a "Million MAGA March" on November 14, 2020 to advocate for the former President and speak out against "fraudulent voting." PID assessed that civil disobedience was possible if counterprotests attempted to interrupt or antagonize the march.
November 12, 2020	Secret Service PID	*Protective Intelligence Brief: Proud Boys Talking Points* This brief provided information about the Proud Boys, including past clashes with left-wing groups and reports of social media posts attributed to the Proud Boys including threats of violence and calls for American citizens to form armed militias to "protect" their rights to free and fair elections.
Park Police		
November 10, 2020	Park Police Intelligence and Counter-terrorism Branch	*Intelligence Briefing: 14 November 2020 Demonstration Activity* This briefing provided information about the MAGA demonstrations being planned in D.C. on November 14, 2020 and assessed there is a high probability of violence if protest and counterprotest groups are allowed to come into direct contact.
Capitol Police		
November 11, 2020	Capitol Police Intelligence and Interagency Coordination Division (IICD)	*Information Paper: Million MAGA March in Washington, D.C. - November 14, 2020* This paper assessed that domestic extremists or violent opportunists may attach themselves to otherwise peaceful demonstrations and that the planned presence of Proud Boys increased the likelihood of violence between them and counterprotesters who planned to attend.
November 12, 2020	Capitol Police IICD	*Information Paper: Million MAGA March in Washington, DC - November 14, 2020 – Update* This paper provided an update about the planned demonstrations and attendees—such as a white supremacist leader and leaders of far-right groups, including the Proud Boys and Oathkeepers—as well as counterprotest groups and their history of civil disobedience and violence against police.
Postal Inspection Service		
November 10, 2020	Postal Inspection Service	*Situational Awareness Bulletin* This bulletin identified the planned demonstration. It noted the event had been reposted within a conservative "Stop the Steal" forum, where analysts identified multiple posts of a violent nature, including threats against Antifa and Black Lives Matter groups and calls for "Patriots" to be armed.

Source: GAO analysis of agency information. | GAO-23-106625

Note: For the purpose of this report, we refer to all of the federal entities in our scope as federal agencies.

Make America Great Again (MAGA) II Demonstrations Threat Products

In December 2020, five federal agencies developed at least five threat products related to the MAGA II demonstrations on December 12, 2020.[5] The agencies developed the threat products based, in part, on open source information. Threat products included event pre-briefs and information papers that summarized protest-related information for operational use, and other products that assessed potential threats for law enforcement planning purposes. See table 6 for additional information about the agencies' threat products.

Table 6: Summary of Threat Products Developed by Selected Federal Agencies Prior to the Make America Great Again (MAGA) II Demonstrations on December 12, 2020

Date product developed	Responsible entity	Title and summary of threat product
Secret Service		
December 11, 2020	Secret Service Protective Intelligence and Assessment Division (PID)	*Protective Intelligence Brief: March for Trump* This brief provided information about the planned March for Trump demonstrations on December 12, 2020. PID assessed many of the groups are the same that demonstrated on November 14, 2020, where clashes ensued between supporters and opponents of the President, and that clashes between demonstrating groups was likely.
Park Police		
December 9, 2020	Park Police Intelligence and Counter-terrorism Branch	*Event Pre-Brief: 12 December 2020 Washington Metro Area (WMA) Demonstration Activity* This pre-brief included information about the demonstrations and counterdemonstrations planned for December 12, 2020. It stated they will closely mirror the demonstrations on November 14, 2020, and there is a near certainty of violence and property damage if the two groups are allowed to come into direct contact.
Capitol Police		
December 7, 2020	Capitol Police Intelligence and Interagency Coordination Division (IICD)	*Information Paper: MAGA II March in Washington, DC - December 12, 2020* This paper provided details about the planned MAGA II March. It noted more Proud Boys planned to attend this second march and encouraged violence against left-wing protesters on social media. IICD also had concerns about infighting between certain right-leaning groups.
Senate Sergeant at Arms		
December 8, 2020	Senate Sergeant at Arms Office of Risk and Threat Management	*Open Source Review of the Million MAGA March II* This document provided an overview of the open source media about the march and of Capitol Police-permitted events on Capitol grounds. It noted the first march and how demonstrators for and against the former President clashed, resulting in some violence and arrests.
Postal Inspection Service		

[5]The number of threat products and information in the below table are comprised of the threat products we were able to review but may not demonstrate an exhaustive list.

Date product developed	Responsible entity	Title and summary of threat product
December 2, 2020	Postal Inspection Service	*Threat Assessment* This assessment identified that the Proud Boys announced a protest will take place on December 12, 2020 in a social media post, which included videos of violence against Antifa. It described the Proud Boys' techniques, tactics, and procedures and stated if counterprotesters are present, it is very likely for violence to erupt.

Source: GAO analysis of agency information. | GAO-23-106625

Note: For the purpose of this report, we refer to all of the federal entities in our scope as federal agencies. The Senate Sergeant at Arms office performing these activities was previously known as the Open Source Situational Awareness Team and also as the Intelligence and Protective Services.

January 6, 2021 Capitol Attack Threat Products

From December 2020 through January 6, 2021, seven federal agencies developed a total of 27 threat products prior to the January 6, 2021 Capitol attack based, in part, on open source information.[6] Threat products included briefing statements that summarized protest-related information for operational use, and other products that assessed potential threats for law enforcement planning purposes. See table 7 for additional information on the agency threat products.

Table 7: Summary of Threat Products Developed by Selected Federal Agencies Prior to the January 6, 2021 Capitol Attack

Date product developed	Responsible entity	Title and summary of threat product
Federal Bureau of Investigation (FBI)		
January 5, 2021	FBI New Orleans	*Intelligence Information Report* This report was related to January 6 events.
January 5, 2021	FBI Norfolk	*Situational Information Report: Potential for Violence in Washington, D.C. Area in Connection with Planned 'StoptheSteal' Protest on 6 January 2021* This report indicated that potential violence could occur in Washington D.C., in connection with the "StopTheSteal" protest on January 6. In addition, the FBI identified an online thread discussing calls for violence, including a threat to "[spill] blood" of counterprotesters, with calls to "get violent."
Department of Homeland Security (DHS) Office of Intelligence and Analysis (I&A)		

[6]In a previous report, we reported that federal agencies developed 26 threat products for the events of January 6 based on open sources. In this report, we added an additional report that was developed by the FBI based on information from a confidential human source.

Date product developed	Responsible entity	Title and summary of threat product
January 5, 2021	DHS I&A	*Open Source Intelligence Report: Forum user posts findings after scouting locations for those who are armed and coming to events* This report indicated that an individual, potentially a member of the Proud Boys, staked out parking lots of federal buildings to determine how to bring firearms to January 6 events. The individual noted that they were driving through North Dakota armed with enough ammo to "win a small war."
January 5, 2021	DHS I&A	*Open Source Intelligence Report: A Russian-linked organization, the Duran, posted on their affiliated social media platforms, multiple organization articles and videos pertaining to the U.S. on 5 Jan. 2021* This report indicated that a foreign organization urged other users to "squash" elector challenges and posted videos that discussed a strategy involving the Vice President of the United States and sending electors back to states.
Secret Service		
December 31, 2020	Secret Service Protective Intelligence and Assessment Division (PID)	*Protective Intelligence Brief: March for Trump* This brief detailed the multiple demonstrations and counterdemonstrations planned for January 6. It noted the hashtags #WeAreTheStorm, #1776Rebel, and #OccupyCapitols had gained attention and that the former President's supporters had proposed a movement to occupy Capitol Hill. It also assessed that clashes between opposing groups were likely.
January 4, 2021	Secret Service PID	*Protective Intelligence Brief: March for Trump* This brief provided updated information about the demonstrations and counterdemonstrations planned for January 6. It identified social media calls for people to occupy the U.S. Capitol or their state capitols. It also assessed that clashes between opposing groups were likely.
January 4, 2021	Secret Service PID	*Notable Trends and Tactics for Consideration Ahead of Potential Civil Unrest in the National Capital Region* This brief provided an overview of the demonstrations planned for January 6, including expected crowd size, information about the Proud Boys, and observations about the violent tactics used by protesters across the ideological spectrum at recent large-scale demonstrations.
Park Police		
December 28, 2020	Park Police Intelligence and Counter-terrorism Branch (INTEL)	*6 January 2021 — WMA Demonstration Activity* This executive brief highlighted social media indicating events similar to the prior MAGA demonstrations. It cited concerns that individuals may display more aggressive or desperate behavior, as January 6 has been interpreted to be the final opportunity to act on grievances.
December 31, 2020	Park Police INTEL	*31 December 2020 — WMA Daily Law Enforcement Operational Snapshot* This operational snapshot summarized information on a First Amendment demonstration scheduled for January 6. Park Police noted they expect that groups with diametrically opposed beliefs will be present and, if groups come into close contact, violence is almost certain.
January 1, 2021	Park Police INTEL	*1 January 2021 — WMA Daily Law Enforcement Operational Snapshot* The operational snapshot noted that conditions continue to evolve, with a "main event" on the Ellipse. Social media reports that various groups plan to meet at the U.S. Capitol, among other places. It also noted the "Million MAGA March" may draw individuals from other, smaller rallies.

Date product developed	Responsible entity	Title and summary of threat product
January 3, 2021	Park Police Special Events Unit	*Briefing Statement* The briefing statement noted that First Amendment demonstrations on January 6 will be similar to the MAGA I and MAGA II demonstrations. The statement noted that, in both instances, widespread violence occurred in D.C.
January 4, 2021	Park Police INTEL	*4 January 2021 — WMA Daily Law Enforcement Operational Snapshot* The operational snapshot noted that the then President posted on Twitter that he planned to attend the permitted event at the Ellipse. According to the snapshot, more protesters and counterprotesters plan to attend the event, because of the post. Park Police noted that the probability of violent actions is likely, if opposing groups come into contact with each other.
January 5, 2021	Park Police INTEL	5 January 2021 — WMA Daily Law Enforcement Operational Snapshot The operational snapshot noted that the Proud Boys leader was arrested on January 4 and it is unknown what effect the arrest will have on group members. It stated that the leader was known to keep more violent factions "under control." As of January 5, Park Police deemed none of the reports on social media posts calling for violence to be credible.
January 6, 2021	Park Police INTEL	*6 January 2021 — WMA Daily Law Enforcement Operational Snapshot* The operational snapshot noted that the events of January 5 concluded without issues, while four firearms were uncovered near the Freedom Plaza. Later in the evening, there was a disturbance between police and demonstrators at the Black Lives Matter Plaza.
Capitol Police		
December 23, 2020	Capitol Police Intelligence and Interagency Coordination Division (IICD)	*Intelligence Assessment: January 6, 2021 Joint Session of Congress Demonstrations* The assessment noted that there are planned demonstrations that call for an election overturn. Groups participating in demonstrations are expected to gather at the U.S. Capitol and other locations in D.C. It also noted that some participants plan to be armed on January 6.
December 28, 2020	Capitol Police IICD	*Special Event Assessment: Joint Session of Congress - Electoral College Vote Certification* The assessment indicated that participants from the MAGA I and II events plan to attend demonstrations and that events scheduled to occur on Capitol grounds were generally of low concern. While there is no specific information to indicate violence or civil unrest, it is anticipated confrontations among opposing groups will occur.
December 29, 2020	Capitol Police IICD	*Information Paper: Planned Protests in Washington, DC - December 30, 2020* The paper noted that participants from the MAGA I and II events plan to attend demonstrations and that they engaged in violence with counterprotesters. Violent or controversial events in other cities could spark potentially violent protests in D.C., and domestic extremists may attach themselves to demonstrations.
December 30, 2020	Capitol Police IICD	*Information Paper: Planned Protests in Washington, DC - December 30, 2020* The paper indicated that members of the Proud Boys plan to attend "incognito," while there were no specific counterprotests. The report contained the same threat statement for potentially violent protests and domestic extremists potentially attaching themselves to demonstrations.
December 31, 2020	Capitol Police IICD	*Information Paper: Planned Protests in Washington, DC - December 31, 2020* The paper noted that while there were no planned protests for January 1, 2021, there were no additional protests planned since the previous assessment. It contained the same threat statement for potentially violent protests and domestic extremists potentially attaching themselves to demonstrations.

Date product developed	Responsible entity	Title and summary of threat product
January 3, 2021	Capitol Police IICD	*Special Event Assessment: Joint Session of Congress - Electoral College Vote Certification* The assessment reported that events on January 6, such as the "StopTheSteal" protest, may lead to a significantly dangerous situation for law enforcement and the general public, as supporters of the former President could see January 6 as their last opportunity to overturn the election results. Further, the sense of desperation may lead to violence, and the targets of supporters are not necessarily counterprotesters, but rather Congress itself.
January 4, 2021	Capitol Police IICD	*Information Paper: Planned Protests in Washington, DC - January 5, 2021* The paper reported that participants from the MAGA I and II events plan to attend demonstrations and previously engaged in violence with counterprotesters. It contained the same threat statement for potentially violent protests and domestic extremists potentially attaching themselves to demonstrations.
January 5, 2021	Capitol Police IICD	*Information Paper: Planned Protests in Washington, DC - January 6, 2021* The paper provided an overview of protests to be held on Capitol grounds related to the counting of electoral votes, where the Million MAGA March will take place at the Freedom Plaza and Ellipse. Participants from the prior MAGA marches plan to attend the demonstrations and previously engaged in violence with counterprotesters. The report contained the same threat statement for potentially violent protests and domestic extremists potentially attaching themselves to demonstrations.
Senate Sergeant at Arms		
December 21, 2020	Senate Sergeant at Arms Office of Risk and Threat Management	*Open Source Review of January 6, 2021 Planned Demonstration Activity* The open source review indicated that Tweets by the former President were encouraging a demonstration in D.C. It identified that turnout reported for previous MAGA demonstrations was lower, but multiple acts of violence occurred after groups clashed.
December 30, 2020	Senate Sergeant at Arms Office of Risk and Threat Management	*Open Source Review of January 6, 2021 Planned Demonstration Activity* The open source review indicated that members of the Proud Boys planned to attend the events of January 6 "incognito."
January 4, 2021	Senate Sergeant at Arms Office of Risk and Threat Management	*Open Source Review of January 6, 2021 Planned Demonstration Activity* The open source review indicated that more posts on Parler by the Proud Boys show that members plan to attend in record numbers.
Postal Inspection Service		
December 22, 2020	Postal Inspection Service	*Million MAGA March - Round III* The threat assessment indicated that individuals planning to attend the "Million MAGA March" on January 6 posted about potential violence. One post urged "fellow patriots and oath keepers" to "take up your arms…and hang every traitor."
December 30, 2020	Postal Inspection Service	*Wimkin and the Million Militia March* The situational awareness bulletin identified a new social media platform, Wimkin, used in place of Parler and Gab generally by militia groups. These groups discussed attending the "Million Militia March," where individuals stated that they should treat counterprotesters as enemy combatants, noting "there will be blood."

Source: GAO analysis of agency information. | GAO-23-106625

Note: For the purpose of this report, we refer to all of the federal entities in our scope as federal agencies. The Senate Sergeant at Arms office performing these activities was previously known as the Open Source Situational Awareness Team and also as the Intelligence and Protective Services.

Appendix V: Comments from the Department of Justice

U.S. Department of Justice

Federal Bureau of Investigation

Washington, D.C. 20535-0001

January 10, 2023

Ms. Triana McNeil
Director
Homeland Security and Justice Team
Government Accountability Office
441 G Street, NW
Washington, DC 20548

Dear Ms. McNeil:

The Federal Bureau of Investigation (FBI) appreciates the General Accounting Office's (GAO) coordination and collaboration in drafting this report. The FBI accepts both recommendations and looks forward to updating GAO on its progress as we work toward resolving these recommendations.

We also appreciate the opportunity to share our views on the FBI's efforts related to the events of January 6 and some highlights in the report. The FBI's efforts on January 6 fell into three main categories: intelligence collection, intelligence sharing, and tactical assistance for law enforcement partners.

First, the FBI sought and collected intelligence including information posted online or collected from other FBI field offices throughout the country. As the GAO report notes, "[i]n the weeks preceding the January 6 attack on the Capitol, the FBI obtained information across other sources indicating potential threats. Through human source reporting, investigations, and observed activity, the FBI identified the increasing threat of violence at high profile special events, such as the 2020 election and 2021 presidential inauguration."[1] In fact, throughout 2020, the FBI issued approximately a dozen external intelligence products to our partners specifically raising concerns about domestic violent extremism—including concerns about domestic violent extremism related to the election and related to domestic violent extremism continuing past election day itself right up to the time of the certification and the inauguration. The GAO report notes that the FBI was one of two federal agencies who identified credible threats and took investigative action to address the threats related to the events of January 6.[2]

Second, the FBI continuously shared intelligence with our partners in the National Capital Region (NCR) through multiple avenues, including frequent phone calls, scheduled

[1] Government Accountability Office, [GAO], *Capitol Attack: Federal Agencies Identified Some Threats, but Did Not Fully Process and Share Information Prior to January 6, 2021*, 20-21 (2022).

[2] *Id.* at 23.

Ms. Triana McNeil

meetings, email, and the establishment of command posts both at the Washington Field Office and FBI Headquarters. The GAO report highlighted the fact that "the FBI developed approximately 25 Guardian reports and assessments regarding unrest related to the election certification…."[3] The GAO further noted several specific instances where the FBI shared information from Guardian reports with partners prior to the January 6, 2021 attack, including on January 5, 2021, when "the FBI shared two reports it developed regarding individuals planning to engage in violence against law enforcement and members of Congress with partners, including DHS and Capitol Police."[4] Through these products, raw intelligence was shared with federal, state, and local partners warning of the threat posed by domestic violent extremists, including the potential for increased violent extremist activity at lawful protest events.

Third, based on the intelligence then available to the FBI, we pre-positioned tactical teams and specialized resources to respond to requests for assistance from our partners who were primarily responsible for physical security in the NCR, including the Capitol.

CONCLUSION

We appreciate the GAO's extensive fact gathering and thorough analysis in the report. As the FBI works diligently to address the recommendations in the GAO's report, we will incorporate GAO's conclusion that, despite collecting and sharing significant pieces of threat reporting, the FBI did not process all relevant information related to potential violence on January 6.[5]

The FBI continues to be introspective regarding its role in sharing intelligence regarding the events of January 6. Our goal is always to disrupt and stay ahead of the threat, and we are constantly trying to learn and evaluate what we could have done better or differently, this is especially true of the attack on the Capitol. While the FBI and our law enforcement partners were aware of and certainly planned for a response to potential violence in the NCR on January 6, the FBI was not aware of actionable intelligence indicating that a large mob would storm the Capitol building. It is worth emphasizing that the findings of the GAO do nothing to dispute that assertion.

Sincerely,

Larissa L. Knapp
Executive Assistant Director
National Security Branch

[3] *Id.* at 29.

[4] *Id.*

[5] *Id.* at 25.

Appendix VI: Comments from the Department of Homeland Security

U.S. Department of Homeland Security
Washington, DC 20528

February 16, 2023

Triana McNeil
Director, Homeland Security and Justice
U.S. Government Accountability Office
441 G Street, NW
Washington, DC 20548

Re: Management Response to Draft Report GAO-23-106625, "CAPITOL ATTACK: Federal Agencies Identified Some Threats, but Did Not Fully Process and Share Information Prior to January 6, 2021"

Dear Ms. McNeil:

Thank you for the opportunity to comment on this draft report. The U.S. Department of Homeland Security (DHS or the Department) appreciates the U.S. Government Accountability Office's (GAO) work in planning and conducting its review and issuing this report.

DHS leadership is pleased to note GAO's recognition of the role that the Department's Office of Intelligence and Analysis (I&A) plays in sharing intelligence and analysis with operators and decisionmakers across all levels of government to identify and mitigate threats to the homeland. Specifically, GAO noted that prior to January 6, 2021, I&A had written policies addressing the collection, documentation, and sharing of threat information. Furthermore, DHS I&A collected and shared information regarding potential threats to January 6 events with law enforcement partners, and also deployed additional personnel for information-sharing and support the day of the attack. DHS remains committed to identifying and sharing information on potential threats to equip the Department and its stakeholders with timely intelligence and information needed to keep the homeland safe, secure, and resilient.

The draft report contained ten recommendations, including four for DHS with which the Department concurs. Enclosed find our detailed response to each recommendation. DHS previously submitted technical comments addressing several accuracy, contextual, and other issues under a separate cover for GAO's consideration.

Again, thank you for the opportunity to review and comment on this draft report. Please feel free to contact me if you have any questions. We look forward to working with you again in the future.

Sincerely,

JIM H CRUMPACKER Digitally signed by JIM H CRUMPACKER Date: 2023.02.16 12:40:46 -05'00'

JIM H. CRUMPACKER, CIA, CFE
Director
Departmental GAO-OIG Liaison Office

Enclosure

2

Enclosure: Management Response to Recommendations Contained in GAO-23-106625

GAO recommended that the Under Secretary for I&A:

Recommendation 3: Assess the extent to which its internal controls ensure personnel follow existing and updated policies for processing open source threat information.

Response: Concur. In fiscal year (FY) 2021, the then-Acting Under Secretary for I&A provided policy guidance to the workforce on May 7, 2021 establishing the need for a robust Internal Controls Program (ICP) to ensure appropriate Departmental and Federal requirements are met on time. Accordingly, on September 30, 2021, the I&A Chief Financial Officer (CFO) established an Internal Controls Branch (ICB) to develop the ICP and implement appropriate control and measurement mechanisms for organizational accountability. In FY 2022 ICB began the process of gathering the foundational data necessary to establish a systematic processes for assessing I&A's non-financial activities, to include controls related to sharing of open source threat information with external partners.

Upon completion of the data gathering, ICB will assess I&A's critical non-financial operations to ensure I&A's operational controls are designed in compliance with laws and regulations to serve as an established foundation for I&A's operations. Estimated Completion Date (ECD): September 29, 2023.

Recommendation 4: Following its assessment, implement a plan to address any internal control deficiencies identified to ensure personnel consistently follow the policies for processing open-source threat information.

Response: Concur. In FY 2022 ICB implemented a Corrective Action Program to develop Corrective Action Plans (CAPs) for assessment identified deficiencies. Specifically, CAPs created under this program consist of root cause analysis, remediation milestones with due dates, and follow-up actions that are reported to I&A's Senior Leadership on a quarterly basis.

Upon completion of the open source operational assessments, ICB will work with stakeholders to develop CAPs to address all policy and procedural deficiencies related to open source threat information. ECD: December 29, 2023.

Recommendation 5: Assess the extent to which its internal controls ensure personnel consistently follow the policies for sharing threat-related information with relevant agencies such as Capitol Police.

3

Response: Concur. As previously noted, the then-Acting Under Secretary for I&A provided policy guidance to the workforce in FY 2021 establishing the need for a robust ICP to ensure appropriate Departmental and Federal requirements are met on time. Subsequently, I&A established an ICB to develop the ICP and implement appropriate control and measurement mechanisms for organizational accountability. Once ICB completes gathering the foundational data necessary to establish a systematic process for assessing I&A's non-financial activities, ICB will assess I&A's critical non-financial operations to ensure I&A's operational controls are designed in compliance with laws and regulations to serve as an established foundation for I&A's operations. ECD: September 29, 2023.

Recommendation 6: Following its assessment, implement a plan to address any internal control deficiencies identified to ensure personnel consistently follow the policies for sharing threat-related information with relevant agencies such as Capitol Police.

Response: Concur. As previously noted, ICB implemented a Corrective Action Program to develop CAPs to address deficiencies identified by assessment findings, which consist of root cause analysis, remediation milestones with due dates, and follow-up actions that are regularly reported to I&A's Senior Leadership.

Upon completion of the threat-related information sharing operational assessments, ICB will work with stakeholders to develop CAPs to deficiencies identified. ECD: December 29, 2023.

4

Appendix VII: Comments from the U.S. Capitol Police

PHONE: 202-224-9806

UNITED STATES CAPITOL POLICE

OFFICE OF THE CHIEF
119 D STREET, NE
WASHINGTON, DC 20510-7218

December 16, 2022

COP 221801

Ms. Triana McNeil
Director
Government Accountability Office
Homeland Security and Justice
Washington, DC 20226

Dear Ms. McNeil:

This letter is in response to the recommendations made within the draft report titled *Capitol Attack: Federal Agencies Identified Some Threats; but Did Not Fully Process and Share Information Prior to January 6, 2021.* The Department agrees with the recommendation made within this report and we are currently taking steps to implement the below recommendation. Specifically, GAO recommended that the United States Capitol Police (USCP):

1. The Chief of the Capitol Police should establish policies for sharing threat-related information agency-wide. (Recommendation 7 within the report)

Below is the current status of the recommendation.

Recommendation 1: The Chief of the Capitol Police should establish policies for sharing threat-related information agency-wide. (Recommendation 7 within the report)

Department Response December 16, 2022: The Department is currently drafting policy that will provide guidance for sharing threat-related information agency-wide. This policy is currently under executive review.

Thank you for the opportunity to respond to the GAO's recommendation and to provide information on the actions taken in response to the recommendation contained in the report.

Very respectfully,

J. Thomas Manger
Chief of Police

cc: Jason R. Bell, Acting Assistant Chief for Protective & Intelligence Operations
Sean P. Gallagher, Acting Assistant Chief of Police for Uniformed Operations
Yogananda D. Pittman, Acting Chief Administrative Officer
Carol A. Absher, Program Manager / Audit Liaison

Appendix VIII: Comments from the Department of the Interior

United States Department of the Interior

OFFICE OF THE SECRETARY
Washington, DC 20240

Ms. Triana McNeil
Director, Homeland Security and Justice
U.S. Government Accountability Office
441 G Street, NW
Washington, DC 20548

Dear Ms. McNeil:

Thank you for providing the Department of the Interior (Department) an opportunity to review and comment on the draft Government Accountability Office (GAO) report titled, *Capitol Attack: Federal Agencies Identified Some Threats, but Did Not Fully Process and Share Information Prior to January 6, 2021* (GAO-23-104793SU). The National Park Service (NPS) generally agrees with the findings and concurs with the recommendations.

We appreciate GAO's review of NPS policies and practices related to intelligence sharing. The GAO issued two recommendations to the Department as part of its overall findings that apply to NPS. Below is the response to the specific recommendations, including the steps the NPS has taken or will be taking to address the concerns raised.

Recommendation 9: The Chief of Park Police should update its policies to clarify how it uses information from other agencies on potential threats of violence.

Response: Concur. An update to the current policies utilized by the U.S. Park Police Intelligence and Counterterrorism Branch was self-initiated soon after the events of January 6, 2021. The final draft of this policy update was submitted to the U.S. Park Police Planning and Development Unit for final review and comments on October 28, 2022. In part, the stated purpose of this policy update is to provide "guidelines and principles for the collection, analysis, and distribution of intelligence information" by the U.S. Park Police.

Target Date: March 2023.

Recommendation 10: The Chief of Park Police should establish a process for determining what threat-related information it shares with NPS permit officials.

Response: Concur. The Commander of the U.S. Park Police Intelligence and Counterterrorism Branch will, by the target date provided, produce written guidelines defining the process by which threat-related information is shared with NPS permit officials. These written guidelines will also address how the U.S. Park Police shares threat-related information with all appropriate NPS officials. These guidelines will be intended to ensure that the appropriate NPS officials are briefed concerning any threats that the U.S. Park Police deems credible and actionable.

Target Date: March 2023.

If you should have any questions or need additional information, please contact Caitlin Rogalski, Chief of the Accountability Office, at caitlin_rogalski@nps.gov or 202-513-7241.

Sincerely,

Date: 2022.12.19
15:45:56 -05'00'

Shannon Estenoz
Assistant Secretary
for Fish and Wildlife and Parks

Appendix IX: GAO Contact and Staff Acknowledgments

GAO Contact

Triana McNeil, Director, Homeland Security and Justice, (202) 512-8777 or McNeilT@gao.gov

Staff Acknowledgments

In addition to the contact named above, Kevin Heinz (Assistant Director), Khaki LaRiviere (Analyst-in-Charge), Imoni Hampton Timberlake, Jennifer Bryant, Kathryn Lenart, Christina Puentes, Jan Montgomery, Mary Turgeon, Amanda Miller, S. Andrew Stavisky, Dominick Dale, Susan Hsu, Eric Hauswirth, James Arp, Taiyshawna Battle, Willie Commons III, Benjamin Crossley, Andrew Curry, Roshni Davé, Clifton Douglas, Elizabeth Dretsch, Maria Edelstein, Michelle Everett, Brett Fallavollita, Gretta Goodwin, Geoffrey Hamilton, Pamela Harris, Delwen Jones, Catina Latham, Steven Lozano, Diana Maurer, Brian Mazanec, Erin O'Brien, Daniel Paepke, Ernest Powell Jr, Kevin Reeves, Malika Rice, Jodie Sandel, Janet Temko-Blinder, Khristi Wilkins, and Melissa Wolf made key contributions to this report.

GAO's Mission

The Government Accountability Office, the audit, evaluation, and investigative arm of Congress, exists to support Congress in meeting its constitutional responsibilities and to help improve the performance and accountability of the federal government for the American people. GAO examines the use of public funds; evaluates federal programs and policies; and provides analyses, recommendations, and other assistance to help Congress make informed oversight, policy, and funding decisions. GAO's commitment to good government is reflected in its core values of accountability, integrity, and reliability.

Obtaining Copies of GAO Reports and Testimony

The fastest and easiest way to obtain copies of GAO documents at no cost is through our website. Each weekday afternoon, GAO posts on its website newly released reports, testimony, and correspondence. You can also subscribe to GAO's email updates to receive notification of newly posted products.

Order by Phone

The price of each GAO publication reflects GAO's actual cost of production and distribution and depends on the number of pages in the publication and whether the publication is printed in color or black and white. Pricing and ordering information is posted on GAO's website, https://www.gao.gov/ordering.htm.

Place orders by calling (202) 512-6000, toll free (866) 801-7077, or TDD (202) 512-2537.

Orders may be paid for using American Express, Discover Card, MasterCard, Visa, check, or money order. Call for additional information.

Connect with GAO

Connect with GAO on Facebook, Flickr, Twitter, and YouTube.
Subscribe to our RSS Feeds or Email Updates. Listen to our Podcasts.
Visit GAO on the web at https://www.gao.gov.

To Report Fraud, Waste, and Abuse in Federal Programs

Contact FraudNet:

Website: https://www.gao.gov/about/what-gao-does/fraudnet

Automated answering system: (800) 424-5454 or (202) 512-7700

Congressional Relations

A. Nicole Clowers, Managing Director, ClowersA@gao.gov, (202) 512-4400, U.S. Government Accountability Office, 441 G Street NW, Room 7125, Washington, DC 20548

Public Affairs

Chuck Young, Managing Director, youngc1@gao.gov, (202) 512-4800
U.S. Government Accountability Office, 441 G Street NW, Room 7149
Washington, DC 20548

Strategic Planning and External Liaison

Stephen J. Sanford, Managing Director, spel@gao.gov, (202) 512-4707
U.S. Government Accountability Office, 441 G Street NW, Room 7814,
Washington, DC 20548

www.ingramcontent.com/pod-product-compliance
Lightning Source LLC
LaVergne TN
LVHW061248100826
845148LV00008B/1064
9781608881505